the ULTIMATE
SUCCESS FORMULA

the ULTIMATE SUCCESS FORMULA

The Unstoppable System to Achieve
Happiness, Wealth and Freedom!

CARLOS MARIN

NEW YORK

the ULTIMATE SUCCESS FORMULA
The Unstoppable System to Achieve Happiness, Wealth and Freedom!

© 2014 MAVIN SYSTEMS INTERNATIONAL, Ltd

Published in New York, New York, by Morgan James Publishing. Morgan James and The Entrepreneurial Publisher are trademarks of Morgan James, LLC.
www.MorganJamesPublishing.com

The Morgan James Speakers Group can bring authors to your live event. For more information or to book an event visit The Morgan James Speakers Group at www.TheMorganJamesSpeakersGroup.com.

ISBN 978-1-61448-281-9 paperback
Library of Congress Control Number:
2012935938

Cover Photo by:
Maggie Hudson
Honeyphoto11@gmail.com

Interior Design by:
Bonnie Bushman
bonnie@caboodlegraphics.com

In an effort to support local communities, raise awareness and funds, Morgan James Publishing donates a percentage of all book sales for the life of each book to Habitat for Humanity Peninsula and Greater Williamsburg.

Get involved today, visit
www.MorganJamesBuilds.com

Habitat
for Humanity®
Peninsula and
Greater Williamsburg
Building Partner

To the Infinite Power
Which flows through Me and You,
Empowering us to achieve Unlimited Possibilities
According to the level of our Belief,
Whom I Know as
God

and

To Its most Beautiful Manifestation
In the entire Universe to Me...
My Soul Mate
My Partner
My Lover
and
Best Friend
Cecy

CONTENTS

FOREWORD

Carlos Marin has developed huge global marketing organizations of hundreds of thousands of entrepreneurs and helped thousands become financially free. Yet, when I met him, Carlos had signed up for one of my *Train The Trainer*™ Courses.

Now that I've come to know him, it makes perfect sense. Carlos teaches the success principles that have made him a multi-millionaire in live three-day seminars that are massive life transforming experiences. He came to me because he was in search of an even higher level of mentorship. With Carlos there's no slowing down or just staying in place. He always wants to grow and learn and, most of all, to share.

This book grew out of a question Carlos repeatedly asked himself. Indeed, it's a question all of us who are engaged in teaching success principles ask: "Why do some people take the principles that I teach and produce phenomenal results and others simply hear them and don't do anything at all?" Carlos decided to write a book that would be so clear, so unequivocal that whoever read it could not help but be successful. Naturally, some will read the book, nod and agree with what Carlos teaches but not put the Principles into practice. That would be a tragedy because this book will deliver the success it promises.

The Principles of Success on which Carlos bases his teachings are nearly as old as time. In this book, Carlos breaks them down and sets out a practical process that will get you from where you are right now, Point A, to where you truly desire to be, Point B, if you apply it.

Carlos had many obstacles to overcome on his own journey to success. As a young Cuban-American with little in the way of education or a sense of purpose, he was floundering when he encountered Network Marketing. Even then, this man who now speaks to stadium crowds in the thousands couldn't speak to even ten people in a living room.

With each step he took toward financial freedom and personal fulfillment, Carlos looked deeper to find out how he achieved what he did and how best to share it. That's why this book exists and why it's a true "How To" book. Follow the principles and life will improve, and improve beyond what you can presently imagine.

When you meet Carlos Marin within the pages of this book, you will meet the focused, energetic, brilliant person I've come to know. Allow him to become your teacher. You will be forever grateful to him and glad that you took the time to practice what he teaches.

Jack Canfield

America's #1 Success Coach

Author- *Chicken Soup for the Soul* and *The Success Principles*

ACKNOWLEDGEMENTS

I've been in the process of writing this book for almost 20 years now. The biggest problem that I've had in finally publishing it is that, since I'm totally dedicated to personal growth, I'm always learning, growing and evolving as a person, leader and student of Universal Principles. Because I do a lot of public speaking, I'm continually seeking to enhance my understanding and knowledge of these principles so that I can teach them even more effectively.

So, every time I thought I had the Formula perfected, I would have a greater awareness regarding one of the principles and need to start revising again. I finally realized, as John Maxwell stated in his introduction to *The 21 Irrefutable Laws of Leadership,* that his frustration with writing—and mine—is that once a book is published, it freezes in time. What this means is that if we are friends or business associates, and we meet to talk every so often, every time we get together, whether socially or in a mentoring session, I would share with you some new insight, concept or strategy that I had learned or mastered recently, and would in essence one-up (or outdate) my book.

Since I am always seeking to improve and rise to ever-higher levels of consciousness, this process was continually happening and "freezing me!" So, finally, thanks to the continual urgings of my wife, Cecy, who told me that the world needed to hear what I had to say, I decided to publish now and "freeze the book in time." This way, I can continue to write more advanced sequels every year as my consciousness becomes even more enlightened by Universal Truth.

When I started my search for success over 30 years ago, I was pretty frustrated and desperate. I owe my success to a long list of mentors who opened up new worlds to me through their teachings, leading me to master many Universal Principles.

I was very fortunate to get started in network marketing early on in my business career. This industry has afforded me the ability to practice my craft continually by living in the firing line. It has given me a world-wide laboratory of millions of people to test and observe the validity and effectiveness of these Universal Success Principles. I can tell you first hand that they work 100% of the time for 100% of the people who apply them with the right mindset.

It's important that you understand that success is not something you achieve alone. It's a team effort and many coaches and teammates played such a massive role in my success that I can't take all the credit or thank them enough. This may seem like an acceptance speech at the Academy Awards, but I am so grateful for the role they've played in my life that I feel compelled to thank them all publicly.

First of all, I thank my wonderful wife, Cecy, who has believed in me through all the adversities and challenges that have crossed our paths. Even when we were homeless for almost a month, she never doubted me and was lovingly by my side through thick and thin.

We've created a tremendous life together and she's my soul mate, partner, buddy, lover and best friend. She played a tremendous role in helping me put this book together: giving me ideas, collaborating, typing while I dictated, reading, rereading, proofreading, retyping over and over again and being my #1 fan and supporter. If not for her I might still be writing… Thanks Baby, I adore you and am excited to share the rest of our lives together!

Many thanks to my editor, Stephanie DeMizio, who worked tirelessly on this book through all of its iterations and evolutions. I know it's not easy to hit a moving target and because of the aforementioned, this book certainly was one. Thanks to Mary Miller who helped me clarify and organize the spiritual principles outlined in this book in a manner that is understandable and easy to follow. Special thanks to my friend, Chris Gross, who read the manuscript numerous times through its evolution and gave me the input to really make it a primer that helps people understand and apply these powerful principles. And finally, thanks to my proofreader, quality editor and formatter, Lorraine Tegeris, for patiently taking a newbie writer, helping me put it all together and successfully hit our deadlines.

I owe a tremendous debt of gratitude to the DeVos and VanAndel families and the Amway Corporation for the tremendous opportunity they offered me, as well as tens of millions of people throughout the world. It was my first business in the Network Marketing Industry, which afforded me the opportunity to master myself, travel around the world, meet incredible people from many different cultures and fall in love with the human race.

I also must thank all of my mentors in that business for the huge impact they had in my success, I couldn't have done it without you all. Tim Foley was like the big brother I never had. He recruited me into the business, saw the potential in me and had the patience to bring me along until I believed in myself. Bill Childers was the wise patriarch figure in our organization who kept us in line, saw greatness in me (and helped me see it, too) and was an example of incredible humility and unconditional love. Without Bill's belief I probably would have quit 100 times over. I also have to thank Hal Gooch and Dexter Yager for their wisdom and guidance in many phases of my business and for being the original pacesetters of a worldwide organization.

Additionally, many thanks to Kenny Stewart for being the role model and instigator of my awakening to the power I had dormant within, and then challenging me to put it into massive action. Also, thanks to Don Wilson and Randy Haugen for being the master teachers that taught me the strategy of building depth effectively, resulting in a massive global organization. These leaders, and many others too numerous to mention, were the original mentors who taught me the mindset and strategies that made me a millionaire.

The mentoring, leadership and guidance of these mentors empowered me to build a global organization of many hundreds of thousands of active distributors generating billions of dollars in sales revenue, making me millions of dollars and helping to develop over 100 millionaires. Still it wouldn't have been possible without the collaboration of a team of exceptional leaders working as a cohesive unit committed to changing lives.

First of all, thanks to my brothers and sisters in the biz...we grew up together and set out to conquer new worlds with love and passion: Louie and Kathy Carrillo, Terry and Yvonne McEwen, Pedro and Patsy Lizardi, Paul and Carmen Stevens and the late Ivan and Millie Morales.

Heartfelt thanks to all of my European Diamond team especially the late Luis Costa, Chris Costa, Miguel and Pilar Aguado, Emilio and Ana Montarraz, Joaquin and Marian Lucas, Angel and Mayte De

La Calle, Pedro and Ana Valdecantos, Robert and Loli Ritchie, Kike and Adela Martinez, Jose Luis Romero and Isabel Segovia.

Much love and gratitude to my Latin American Diamond team, Estela Salinas, Lourdes Enriquez, Alberto and Lilia Mayagoitia, Lilan and Leonardo DeRodas, Eduardo Barreto, Jose Luis Rabago, Juan Carlos Barrios, Carmen and Tino Hechavarria, Joss Enrique and Gina Rangel, Carlos Valdes, Lilian Valdes, Pepe and Marta Andrade, Consuelo Hernandez, Oscar and Mary Velasco, Joaquin and Maru Maxemin, Mario and Betty Orsini and Nino and Patty Mucciga.

Finally, without my North American team none of this would have gone anywhere. So, special thanks to Jack and Maureen Cerviño, Fernando and Regina Olivar, Armando Alberty, Carlos and Odalys Hechavarria, Wilson and Clelia Lima, Rod and Beth Rees, Jose Rodriguez, Maria Marin-Sanchez, Alfred and Lourdes Rivera, Eddie and Lori Safille and many, many more too numerous to mention.

Without my global executive team most of this wouldn't have been possible either, so thank you Carmen Marin, Ellie Robles, Maria Elena Vasquez, Alejandra Cuirolo de Bisanz, Carlos Santillan, Ignacio Reyes and my right-hand man, VP of Marketing, Raul Garcia who travelled the world helping me manage a global enterprise of nearly 100 employees in nine country offices, servicing over 500,000 distributors in over 30 countries.

I know I've left so many names out and I truly apologize, but I'm limited in the space I have and this could be an entire book of people I have to thank!

I also feel tremendous appreciation and gratitude to Jere Thompson Jr. and Chris Chambless, Co-Founder's of Ambit Energy, my most current venture, for the opportunity they afforded me to do some groundbreaking work marketing a service (electricity and natural gas) through the network marketing model. Their faith in me allowed me to develop a web-based video recruiting and training system that helped take that company from ground floor to over a billion dollars in sales in seven years. Also special thanks to Terry LaCore and John and Terri Hammack for introducing me to Chris and Jere.

No matter how good your systems are they are worthless without great people to deploy and execute them. Special thanks to the other great leaders with whom I collaborated with and worked side-by-side building the Ambit business, especially Brian McClure with whom I spent countless hours the first three years brainstorming strategies to build the business faster and more effectively. Also, many thanks to my friends, leaders and the other nine members of our Top 10 Income Earners Club (The Ten), Steve Thompson, Phillip Eckart, Ray Montie, Chris and Debbie Atkinson, Frank Schmaeling, Esther Spina, Justin and Sherrie Title and Rigoberto Yepez. Getting the business to this level was a team effort and you all were the rock stars who made it happen. You are all huge winners and exceptional role models in our profession.

And thank you to my Ambit Leadership team that has worked to build such a huge organization, Johnny and Fifa Ventura, Aura and Luis Guzman, Cesar and Sonia Baffoni, Cecilia Pizarro, Maria Bautista, Marisol Figueroa, Martha and Leo Ramirez, Doug Rawlins, Jim Denzine, David and Arlyn Belmar, Wilson Montoya, Alfredo Schmidt, Gabriella Aldrete, Elizabeth Jimenez, Maria de Lourdes Cardenas, James and Bonita Hall, Reynaldo Perez, Genaro Aguillon, Miguel Garcia, Ignacio Jasso, Jose Angel and Monica DeAntes, Rafael and Aydee Ramirez, Julius and Shellie Weems, Shantee and Mark McPhee and Assene Moise,. Thanks for all you continue to do!

Most of what I've been able to accomplish would not have been possible without what I have learned from my mentors outside of the network marketing industry: Tony Robbins, who taught me how to identify and transform limiting beliefs into empowering ones, and how to understand the values that were driving and shaping my life, redefine them and re-create my destiny on purpose. The late, great Jim Rohn, who taught me that if I will work as much on myself as I do on my business I will have all the happiness, success and wealth that I could ever desire. Jim, I'll never forget you for that invaluable advice that has served me so well. Dennis Waitley, who taught me the power of focus and that we only get in life what we expect. In case you didn't know, I became known as Mr. Focus due to your advice. Brian Tracy, who turned me on to accelerated learning techniques and opened my mind to a whole new world of quantum learning. John Maxwell, who taught me the Laws of Leadership and the rule of five, which has become a mainstay in my curriculum. Kenneth Copeland, who taught me the power of faith and how to build it to mountain moving heights. Alex Mandossian, who taught me how to do Tele-Seminars and introduced me to the online marketing world, your strategies have definitely made me be exponentially more productive, my friend. Bob Proctor introduced me to the concept of Universal Principles being scientific fact, and taught me how to use them to create my own reality and transform my life. Mary Morrissey, who showed me how to expand my vision to infinite new heights and to expect to receive "this or something better still"... and I am! Jack Canfield, who with his wisdom, mastery and humor taught me to truly embody these principles and teach them at a level I never had before. Thank you, Jack, I'm so honored to have you as my mentor, coach and friend. Brendon Burchard, thank you brother, for all you've taught me about the expert space, online marketing and how to take high performance to a whole new level in my life and the lives of others. Your mentoring over the past two years has been invaluable and is 10Xing my business. I look forward to collaborating with you all in the future as we continue our journey to empower people all over the world.

Finally, thanks to my mom and dad, Zuly and Carlos Marin Sr., who have been shining examples of love, honesty, integrity, humility and even when I didn't want to... always taught me to do the right thing.

And last but not least... Thanks to my children, Allison, Samantha, Janette, Cecy Jr., Andy and Cassie, for all I have learned from you. I apologize for all the times I screwed up while trying to raise you and in the process wound up teaching you my fears, doubts and limitations. Hopefully, you are learning these new and infinitely better lessons that I am teaching today, and overcoming my shortcomings. I love you all with all my heart!

WHY YOU NEED THIS BOOK

Man is buffeted by circumstances so long as he believes himself
to be the creature of outside conditions, but when he realizes that
he is a creative power, and that he may command the hidden soil
and seeds of his being out of which circumstances grow, he then
becomes the rightful master of himself.

—James Allen, As a Man Thinketh

Is it possible to completely control your future and get everything you want in life? Is there a way to guarantee success? What if it was as simple as following a formula? Sound too good to be true? It's not!

Anyone can achieve any success they desire in any area of life. But what it ultimately comes down to is this: How *much* success do you truly want? How much do you feel you can handle? How much success do you feel you deserve? How much are you worthy of having?

Your answers to these questions represent what you will allow and what you will attract into your life. Sure, there are a multitude of factors at play on your path to success and happiness. Thousands of books have been written on success over the years as well as countless biographies of people who have made an impact on this world.

In these books, in our culture, in our families and businesses, innumerable qualities, characteristics and strategies have been credited with creating high-level success in business and in life. A big dream, clear vision, burning desire, persistence, tenacity, determination, singleness of purpose, people skills, massive action, goal setting and even being at the right place at the right time have been named as the key secret to success, depending on who is telling the story.

Maybe you've heard that success is based on:

- Luck
- Discipline
- Hard Work
- Paying Your Dues
- Sacrifice
- Selling Your Soul

Sound familiar? I bet in the course of your life you've tried a few of these "strategies." I've tried them all. They did not make me wealthy and they certainly did not make me happy.

I'm going to let you in on *my* secret. *Success is not hit and miss.* It is based on the systematic execution of principles that are as reliable as gravity.

What do a multi-award winning musician, all-star athlete or bestselling author have in common? Besides amazing gifts, talents and drive, they all have mastered some type of formula that brings them repeated success. How about the couple that has been happily married for 50 years, the lifetime marathon runner or the entrepreneur who has built multi-million dollar businesses over and over again? They all produce definite, quantifiable results that are consistently replicable.

I believe you can be, do and have anything that you want in life. The only requirement is that you develop the mindset and use the strategies of the person who already is, does and has it.

In that last 30 years, I have built multiple marketing organizations that have generated billions of dollars in sales revenues and I have helped recruit and train several million entrepreneurs worldwide. Why do I tell you this? Because anyone can do what I've done; there is nothing more special about me than you or anyone else. I just know and apply the formula to continually create my best life with clear intent, focus, passion and daily action. And you can, too.

The minute you gain control of your mind and thoughts and direct your action purposely and with conviction, you will produce the results you desire. I know this because I've used the principles I'm about to teach you in my own life, plus taught them to others, and they have worked time and time again. At the age of 57 years old, I am in better shape now than I was in my 30s. I am in a phenomenal relationship with my soul mate. I am blessed with six beautiful children and two amazing grandchildren. I am financially free. And most of all, I am living my purpose of sharing what I know with you and with the world.

My wife, Cecy, and I (age 33 and 39)...Cecy and I (age 51 and 57)

Having worked with millions of people in 40 countries through my success development and training programs, I've learned that the biggest reason people fail—in work, relationships and their health—is because they focus on strategy, tactics or mechanics, without developing a success mindset.

Have you ever heard this before, or better yet, have you been the one to say it? "That _____ doesn't work for me." Whatever it is. That exercise program. Eating plan. Business technique. Investment tool. Whatever it is, do you have the tendency to shut it down before you even begin? Or worse, do you actually give it a try, all the while thinking there's no way it will work?

If you have the right mindset you will figure out the strategy. **What you feel you are worthy of is the determining factor in creating the life of your dreams**...to actually having it unfold almost effortlessly within your experience.

The key is to understand who you really are, the unlimited potential and power within you and the good things you absolutely deserve to have. Then and only then can you truly make your life the masterpiece that you were put here to create.

Chapter 1

THE ULTIMATE SUCCESS FORMULA

What you focus on, imagine, commit to and act on with faith you will manifest in your life!

—**Carlos Marin**

My Story

In 1982, I was 25 years old, lost, confused and depressed. As a Cuban immigrant who had been raised in a middle class family and educated by loving and well-meaning parents, teachers, coaches and clergy, I grew up believing that outside conditions determined my fate.

I was born in Cuba, the day after Fidel Castro went into the Sierra Madre Mountains to begin the revolution. The mood in the country, and in my family, was one of fear and apprehension. My parents were so concerned about guerilla fighting breaking out that they went to the hospital early. Would the fear and instability that surrounded my family when I was born affect me later in life?

Castro took over the country in December of 1959, when I was three years old. Shortly thereafter he started taking people's homes, land and belongings. In my parents' neighborhood, the military came to take one of their friend's houses and when he refused, they just shot him dead, point blank, right in front of his family.

Think about all of the turmoil, negativity and violence that happened during the first years of my life. I was surrounded by uncertainty and fear as my parents tried to figure out what to do. "Do we leave? Do we stay a little longer and see what happens? What will happen to us? What will happen to our children?"

They applied for visas to Spain, the United States and Costa Rica, intent on getting out of the country as quickly as possible. The visa from Spain came first, so they prepared to leave.

My little sister got sick with a fever a few days before we were supposed to go and although my parents were afraid that traveling would make her worse, my grandfather insisted we leave immediately, while we still could.

My parents, my sisters and I left everything behind and fled from Cuba with only the clothes we were wearing, one suitcase and a $1,000 bill my father had smuggled out in the heel of his shoe. We began a new life in Spain and subsequently came to the United States a year later.

These experiences affected me negatively for years without my realizing it. I was too young to understand dictatorships or communism, but I still had to leave everything behind, even people

I loved, and move to a strange place. My parents, of course, knew exactly what was happening. They saw everything they and my grandfather (who had labored for over 50 years) had worked for taken from them, literally overnight. This sense of insecurity was pervasive in our household and became part of my consciousness, although I didn't realize how powerful this deep-seated fear of loss was until years later.

While those fears were a motive for my working hard and striving to get ahead in life, at the same time they produced the sensation that somehow I would lose my wealth the same as my grandfather and my parents had. They believed — and unknowingly taught me to believe — that no matter how hard you work, or how much wealth you are able to accumulate, someone can come along and take it all from you.

Fast forward to 1982, I was married, broke and in debt. I was in the insurance business; I owned a property and casualty agency along with a partner and made about $30,000 a year. I rented a small apartment, but drove a BMW I couldn't afford so that I could give the impression of being successful. I was falling deeper and deeper into the hole, with no idea how to turn my life around. I was smoking and drinking, frustrated and ready to give up on life.

I hated my situation and deep inside I had a nagging sensation that there had to be more to life than the depressing conditions in which I was living. I felt that there was a reason I was here and I was determined to find out what that was. Due to my intense desire to change my circumstances, I met a successful businessman through a friend of my wife that showed me a lucrative network marketing opportunity. He also introduced me to some multi-millionaires who were mentoring him who said they'd also teach me what they had done to achieve their success and wealth. They became my first mentors and they introduced me to a curriculum that I never knew existed—the Universal Principles of Success and Wealth.

I consumed these principles as if my life depended on them (which in retrospect, it did). I had such an insatiable hunger for knowledge that I started attending monthly seminars, reading as many books on success as I could find and listening to the audiotapes of people who were living examples of the power of these principles. I learned that success does not come about by accident or luck, but is the result of thinking and acting according to these principles. I also realized that this process could be learned by anyone.

It was challenging at first, because due to my victim mentality and habitual focus on what was wrong in my life, I was still attracting unwanted results and experiences. I was misusing the Laws of Success and suffering the consequences. The first moment of clarity came to me when I realized I could change my life, but had to first change my thinking. Willpower alone would not do it. I had to take complete responsibility and *own* my life—the good and the bad.

To fully own my life, I had to make some important choices. My partner in the insurance agency was not happy about my split-focus between insurance and another business, so I sold my part of the agency and got out. I was not making enough money in network marketing yet to support my family, so I went into energy conservation and management with a friend of mine who was a successful mechanical engineer. While generating income in this new business, I stayed plugged into the system in network marketing because the training and mentoring I was receiving on Universal

Principles was the best available anywhere. The good news was that I was applying all of the success principles I was learning to my energy business and in the course of three years, I was making almost three times as much as I did in insurance! Now I couldn't quit even if I wanted to; I had to stay plugged into this Success System and keep learning more.

In early 1986, I attended a leadership seminar. The speaker told us how he had gone from the verge of bankruptcy to building a business worth millions of dollars, all in the space of two-and-a-half years. He shared his formula for success with us and I really related to this guy because he was young, excited and confident. I decided right there and then that I was going to become a better student of success and use that formula to become a millionaire, too.

The original formula I learned that day was made up of four simple steps:

1. Define your dream.
2. Get a vehicle.
3. Make a plan of action.
4. Take massive action.

It took me more than twice as long as that speaker from the seminar, but in six years, through continued study and practice of the principles, I mastered the formula, made strategic business decisions and I did it. I became a millionaire!

During this process I modeled the fastest growing leaders, made huge strides within my company and stayed focused on my dream, taking massive action while acting as if I was already a millionaire. I also overcame a poor self-image and many beliefs that had been holding me back. Knowing the formula was one thing, but mastering myself was the key ingredient in my success.

Over the past 30 years, I've tested and refined the four-step formula I originally learned and have expanded it into my own **Ultimate Success Formula**, an eight-step system for reaching your full potential and the most powerful formula ever developed for achieving anything you want in life.

The Ultimate Success Formula

Step One: Own Your Life
Step Two: Design Your Life on Purpose
Step Three: Establish Your Intentions
Step Four: Discover Your Blocks
Step Five: Clear and Align
Step Six: Create an Action Blueprint
Step Seven: Take Inspired Action
Step Eight: Be It!

In this book I will not only show you how to apply the Ultimate Success Formula, I'll also teach you the supporting principles and a systematic application of their strategies that are as powerful as the formula itself.

What I'm sharing with you is not just what I learned in the very beginning of my career, which is superficial by comparison. I'm running you through the whole gamut, all the way to the really powerful principles I've only come to learn in the past several years. I've learned these principles through diligent study, application and experience. Because do you think everything always goes as planned?

That once you learn and implement the formula one time, you're done? Of course not!

Losing Everything—
A Blessing in Disguise

After having made millions of dollars in business, I went through a period of time where I experienced tremendous financial losses from things seemingly beyond my control. I lost millions from foreign currency devaluations, dishonest business partners, bad investments and malicious attacks on my businesses. I lost my multi-million dollar house on the water and my wife, daughter and I were actually homeless for almost a month.

What I couldn't fathom back then was how I could create so much value for other people, teaching and helping so many of them to become financially free, and still lose so much.

In my family's case, the one thing they didn't focus on was the fact that if you created success once, you can do it again. Thank God my study of principles to that point had already led me to create a belief system that said: You might take my material goods but you can't take what created my success, which is my mindset and faith in my unlimited source, which is God within me. My attitude was, 'I'll just recreate it, only this time it'll be bigger than ever and built on an unshakeable foundation!'

In actuality, all of that loss was a blessing in disguise because it made me realize that although I knew many powerful principles, I was just coasting, resting on my laurels so to speak. It was a wake up call that there was still something missing, still more I needed to learn in order to be able to create my life totally by my own design and fulfill my <u>true purpose</u> in life. It was the catalyst that made me go beyond the initial four-step success formula and search deeper into Universal Principles to actually create the Ultimate Success Formula.

Finding and living your true purpose can be very challenging because most of us were taught that we must work hard to make money and then, if there's time left over, we can have fun. The presupposition here is work is something difficult that you dislike or even hate to do and cannot have fun doing. The reality is that making money is really not a problem once you learn that money is just a measure of the value you are providing, and then giving more value than you're paid for. Furthermore, making money when you live your passion is actually easy and fun.

So you see, wherever you are, I've been there. I've been broke and became wealthy and I've lost it all and become a millionaire again. If I can transform my life (multiple times!) to enjoy success, wealth and happiness, then you can, too. I'm going to show you how to make the money, create that security that you seek, but also how to have a fun, happy and balanced life.

Throughout this book I will refer back to and expand on parts of my story to more clearly demonstrate the application of the powerful principles of the formula in real life. It will also become very evident to you that mentors have played a big part in my success. While I have synthesized and systemized everything I've learned into the Ultimate Success Formula, in this book I will reference some of my key mentors, both past and present, and what I learned from them. This way you can obtain additional information from many of the best thought leaders in the world.

I feel totally honored that you have decided to share your time with me and are allowing me to mentor you in what I believe is the most important area of your life: taking control of your own mind and future.

Believe it or not, you've offered me a great opportunity for personal growth in the writing of this book. You see, I'm used to teaching in front of live audiences for many hours per day for several days at a time. Therefore, I have the opportunity to receive feedback from people and make adjustments as I go along. Writing this book has forced me to push myself and stretch farther than ever before and I am grateful to you for this experience. I imagine you reading these pages and I am inspired to give you the best of everything I have. I know some of you will want the detail of *how* everything works, while others will want to skip the philosophy and learn what to do right here, right now. Whichever of those is you, this book will deliver.

Start Where You Are

As we begin this journey together I'd like you to understand that if you're not where you want to be in your life right now, it's totally okay. Very few of us were taught what I'll be sharing with you in this book. So I suggest that you be kind and gentle with yourself and open your mind to the possibilities you'll be exposed to as you continue reading.

In order to steer clear of judgment and condemnation of yourself and others, there are three basic premises that I'd like you to keep in mind:

1. Everyone does the best they can at every moment in time according to their level of awareness.
2. You can't give what you don't have.
3. You don't know what you don't know.

Every one of us came into this world as pure unlimited potential. Then, the people who were entrusted with our care immediately began to protect and train us for what they believed was our own good. They taught us what they thought we needed to learn. In essence, they transferred their own beliefs, complete with all their worries, doubts, fears, failures and limitations, to us. They love us and do the best they can in each moment according to their level of awareness, but they can't give us what they don't have or teach us what they don't know.

You have now begun the process of self-awareness and have chosen to follow your own dreams. Be patient with yourself and those that are closest to you. I promise, a whole new world is about to be revealed to you!

Chapter 2

UNIVERSAL PRINCIPLES

I know this world is ruled by Infinite Intelligence. Everything that surrounds us, everything that exists, proves that there are infinite laws behind it. There can be no denying this fact. It is mathematical in its precision.

—Thomas Edison

My intention is to keep this book practical while still covering the deep principles of life that produce real-world results. To that end, I must give you a little of the philosophic and scientific evidence that supports these principles, however, I will keep it as short as possible and give you practical strategies you can use to produce measurable results in your life immediately.

I came to understand the Universal Principles as unerring science after being introduced to the work of spiritual thought leader and author, Thomas Troward. My friend Chris Gross, publisher of *Networking Times* magazine, gave me one of Troward's books that Bob Proctor had recommended called, *The Edinburgh and Dore Lectures on Mental Science.* While I didn't fully understand this book in the beginning, it began to make me see that everything in the universe functions according to infallible, precise law that is working all the time and by which all results are produced automatically. I then looked to Bob Proctor, considered one of the living masters of the Law of Attraction, for additional information. From Proctor's book, *You Were Born Rich,* and several of his audio programs, I learned I was worthy of success and in fact it was my birthright. Because of the work of both of these two men, my life totally transformed and I began a study of success principles at a whole new level that has brought me to where I am today. So let's dive in so you can benefit from this transformational knowledge, too!

The first concept I'd like you to recognize is that we live in an orderly universe controlled by specific laws. Once you know these laws, you can apply them to get the results you want in any area of life. I'm not talking about governmental or societal law, but something much deeper, derived from the origins of humanity. Whatever your religious or spiritual belief, the core of what we're talking about is relevant to all faiths and cultures.

There are three main laws that guide my life and they date all the way back to Hermetic Law, which is the oldest wisdom philosophy on record, pre-dating the earliest Biblical times. Let's break them down in terms that apply to the reality of our universe today, as proven scientifically through quantum physics, because a basic understanding and consistent application of these principles give you a tremendous amount of power to shape your world.

1. The Principle of Mind
2. The Principle of Correspondence
3. The Principle of Cause and Effect

The Principle of Mind

This principle states that everything in the universe is made from consciousness. Now before your eyes glaze over, I promise we won't get too esoteric here. It simply means that everything is made from energy that is intelligent. This Intelligent Energy is coded with information that makes it appear and behave a certain way in the physical world. Modern science today has proven:

- Everything in the universe is comprised of energy and this energy is infinitely intelligent.
- This energy is equally present at every point in space, at every moment in time.
- This Intelligent Energy cannot be created or destroyed; it simply is and is forever in motion, expanding and creating.

The universe is made up of intelligent, thinking energy that has manifested as physical reality. Even our physical bodies are made from this one substance, which is Intelligent Energy. In essence, we are all individual expressions of God (Higher Power, Divine, Source, Infinite Mind, whatever you choose to call it) and create using the same process and power through our own minds, by our own thoughts.

One quick note, for fairness, continuity and consistency, when referring to Intelligent Energy throughout the book, I will use God and Infinite Intelligence interchangeably. These are the words that resonate with me. I use them daily in my meditations, prayers and visualizations. You can use whatever supports your beliefs, but for the sake of clarity and to cut down on confusion as we dive deeper into the principles, let's use God and Infinite Intelligence.

Now, I have often been criticized for talking so much about God in business and how He is the key to all success. This is really not a religious concept because as the creating power in the universe, God/Infinite Intelligence is present in all of its creation as potential power. It shows itself when we give it expression through our thoughts and actions. It is this power that produces all results and you cannot separate yourself from it no matter how hard you try!

Think of it this way, we always have electricity flowing through our homes but we don't see it until we connect a device to it and turn it on. It could be a TV, refrigerator or air conditioner that when turned on, displays the power of the electricity that is giving it life. Without electricity the device could do nothing, right? It's the same with us!

Since we are extensions of Infinite Intelligence, we function according to the same laws that it uses to create. In fact, we are actually using the power of Infinite Intelligence flowing through our own minds to create everything we produce in our lives. We do this through our consistent thoughts and beliefs. The problem is that the power is always working (turned on) so when we don't direct our thoughts to constructive ends on purpose, we are unconsciously directing that power to destructive ends, which is why so many people are frustrated and produce such poor results. We imagine things we don't want to happen and by doing so bring those to pass according to the degree of our fear.

It is critical to direct our thoughts on purpose and know what we believe and are thinking in the first place. We imagine what we desire and according to the clarity of our intentions and degree of our belief, we produce results. However, the strength and clarity of our beliefs are the variables that dictate the timing, from instantaneous to painfully slow, of the physical materialization of our desires.

Whatever you believe to be true is continually produced in your life. As you believe, it is done unto you! This is the Law of Belief, which is the operating system of the Principle of Mind. In his groundbreaking book, *The Biology of Belief*, renowned cell biologist, Bruce H. Lipton, PhD, demonstrates how the new science of epigenetics is revolutionizing our understanding of the link between mind and matter, demonstrating that our thoughts and beliefs actually alter our DNA. What's great is that positive thoughts and beliefs are at least 10 times more powerful than negative ones, so you can transform your life much faster than you may realize, once you are consistent. The more you align with Infinite Intelligence, the stronger your belief and faith and the quicker you produce results.

The Principle of Correspondence

This principle states that there is always a corresponding relationship between the mental and physical planes of existence. I've taught my children for the past 15 years, "As within so without, as without so within." This means that Infinite Intelligence within you is always expressing its creative power. You and I give that power direction by our thoughts, assumptions and beliefs. Your outer world always reflects what's in your inner world (your inner states). Your inner world always produces what it contains in your physical world as results and conditions.

You can easily tell by the results someone is producing in any area of their life, the mindset they have in that area. In other words, if a person is exhibiting the results of failure or lack of love, health, happiness or any positive result in their lives, then they have a failure or lack mentality in the corresponding area. Conversely, if a person is exhibiting the results of success and abundance in any area, then they have a mindset of success and abundance in the corresponding area. A thorough understanding of this principle is a tremendous advantage that will benefit you in all human interactions and business situations.

The Principle of Cause and Effect

The Principle of Cause and Effect states that every cause produces an effect and every effect has its cause. All action is preceded by thought whether conscious and intentional or unconscious and automatic. Everything in the universe happens according to law. Chance, luck or coincidences are only names we give to the results produced by Universal Principles that we don't recognize or understand.

All causes are thoughts and ideas. Our persistent thoughts, ideas and beliefs are what determine our actions and produce every physical or material result (effect) in our lives.

The things most of us strive for in this world are all effects — money, homes, cars, vacations, physical health, recognition and success. Even what we call love, sex and great relationships are all effects. They are the material expressions of thoughts, concepts and ideas. Feelings and emotions are also effects, as they are energetic sensations in our bodies caused by our persistent thoughts.

What about the Law of Attraction?

The Law of Attraction has been very trendy lately, but it's also been improperly taught and highly misunderstood and therefore a source of frustration for many people. If only it was as easy as merely wishing for what you want!

The Law of Attraction is a fundamental law of physics and is the way material effects are produced. In actuality, it's an aspect of and the operating system for the Principle of Cause and Effect.

Like attracts like — that's it. Things that are like each other are drawn together.

The Law of Attraction is an absolute and impersonal law. It has nothing to do with your personality, your religion, being a good or bad person or anything else. It's a changeless law of the universe, as certain as gravity. You don't need to understand how the law of gravity works in order to keep yourself from flying off into the stratosphere and the same thing applies to the Law of Attraction.

The first time I heard of the Law of Attraction I thought it had to do with male/female relationships or how opposite poles attract (which is the Law of Magnetism, a totally different law). But, just because I didn't understand this law didn't mean it wasn't working in my life. In retrospect, I realize I had attracted into my life the results that were precisely congruent with my thoughts and belief system. I had a negative attitude, which attracted negative results. As soon as I began to adjust my mindset and develop a positive attitude, my results began to improve dramatically.

Every experience, condition and circumstance that you have in your life is attracted and created by you. It's easy to accept that when you're producing positive results, but that's not what people want to hear when they're unhappy with their lives. When people aren't happy with their results, and believe their circumstances are beyond their control, they become really good at attracting a ton of circumstances that they don't want. It's a dangerous cycle.

Many times when I talk about this in my seminars, participants get really upset. Some of them will say, "But wait a minute, my circumstances, my family background, the government, the economy, my company or the situation I'm in are the reasons I am where I am."

I have to confess that I felt this way too when I started learning this stuff and had a really hard time swallowing the fact that I had attracted the crappy circumstances in my life.

Let me get this out of the way now: you no longer need to buy into the victim mentality or succumb to your own "broke" consciousness. You can decide to change it today. Realize that if you think about how unjust life is or how people are always out to get you — that line of thinking will produce injustice in your life. Things will go against you and people will continually take advantage of you.

If you think life is a struggle and you have to fight for everything you get and sacrifice to succeed, you will struggle, fight and compete in order to get your piece of the pie and make all kinds of sacrifices to succeed.

If you're always worried about not having enough money or losing your money, that thinking will produce lack and you will always come up short.

If you think you're unworthy, that you don't deserve (fill in the blank), whether it's love, wealth, health or happiness, whatever you feel unworthy of or undeserving of will elude you all of your life.

While I totally agree that none of us wants to attract these negative experiences on purpose, it doesn't change the fact that we attract them, because at some point we've given them thought or emotion or even feared them. This was the tough realization I arrived at in my own life as I tested the principles and found them to be 100% true.

Make no mistake about it; it's your beliefs and habitual thought patterns that are the power in your life and the real cause of your circumstances. Never underestimate the Law of Belief; the sum total of your beliefs is the reality you are living. It is your beliefs that set your expectations in life, which in turn create your vibration, which is what attracts like results. This is what they didn't explain clearly in the movie, *The Secret,* which is a real shame because I personally know several of the teachers who were featured and they not only know this, they teach it in their programs, too.

How do you start your day? Do you set an alarm? Wake up with the sun? Do you have to be dragged out of bed? Or are you lured out by the smell of freshly brewed coffee that was preset the night before? Many of us don't even think about how we begin each morning, but what we do, cursing the alarm clock, repeatedly hitting the snooze button and frantically getting ready because we're late again, has a significant effect on what we will produce for the rest of the day. By the way, this was me before I began to learn the principles!

Have you ever considered the benefits of starting your day with gratitude? What about ending your day in appreciation, as well? Every morning I count my blessings. I give thanks for another beautiful day, my loved ones, for all the great circumstances in my life. I set my intentions for the day and take a few moments to visualize them. At night, I once again turn to gratitude before I drift off to sleep. Whatever you're going through, you can always find something to appreciate.

It's critical that you understand that you are a creator. You have the choice of what you create by choosing your thoughts. Your life is made up of the minutes in the day and what you're thinking about during all of those minutes. If you consistently control and purposely direct what you're thinking about, you will change your life!

Chapter 3

WELCOME TO YOUR MIND

The mind is everything. What you think you become.

—Buddha

Becoming Conscious

Today you often hear talk about raising your consciousness in order to be more successful, peaceful, happy or joyful, but what does that really mean? What is consciousness anyway? I'll give you a hint: you're increasing yours just by reading this book!

One day, early in my career when I was struggling to gain momentum in business, a mentor of mine introduced me to the work of one of the greatest personal success writers of all time, Napoleon Hill. As I read his classic book, *Think and Grow Rich*, the lights started coming on for me. The first sentence alone states, "Truly thoughts are things and powerful things at that when mixed with purpose, persistence and a burning desire for their translation into riches or other material objects."

I remember when I read that sentence I was shocked and confused. I thought, 'How could something I can't see or touch be a thing?' I didn't realize that energy, although invisible, was a physical thing or that thought was energy coded with specific information that directs our behavior and solidifies it into material objects and conditions.

As I continued to read the book, I began to apply its principles, even though I didn't understand them all. I directed my thoughts toward my goals and did my best not to allow them to ramble to unimportant things like worry, fear or the opinion of others, as hard as that was. As I stayed focused on my goals and what I wanted my life to be like, seeming miracles started happening. In less than two years I was able to sell my energy business for $100,000 and devote myself full time to my network marketing business, which was my strongest desire at that time and was eventually the vehicle that made me a millionaire.

I finally started realizing that thoughts truly are things!

Around this time I was also introduced to the concept of the conscious and subconscious mind and the power of focused imagination, which we're going to talk about next, and I was blown away. I committed myself to a life-long study of the use of the mind to produce success, wealth, love and happiness. As I used my conscious mind purposely to direct my subconscious, the results I produced were beyond fantastic.

Your state of consciousness or as I call it, your mindset, is everything you accept, assume and believe to be true. This inner mental concept of yourself is what produces your outer world and all the conditions within it. So the idea is to open yourself up to a higher level of awareness by exposing yourself to new empowering ideas, ways of thought, outlooks and experiences so that you continue to grow, evolve and appreciate different points of view. Books, movies, seminars, travel, spending time in nature, meditation, using your body athletically or artistically, listening to uplifting music, giving to those less fortunate, connecting with loved ones — these are all ways of elevating your mindset to give you the best possible vision of the world and your place within it.

Key Components of The Mindset

Your mindset is comprised of several major components. This is a rather complex area, but for the sake of simplicity and practical use, we'll break it down into four key components, which impact every area of our lives.

1. **Beliefs:** What you believe to be true, the things you have a sense of certainty about, ideas and concepts you've heard or thought many times and accept as facts. This is your reality.
2. **Identity:** Your self-concept, who you believe you are. This is really just a giant set of beliefs about how you see and feel about *yourself*, but it governs all aspects of your life in such a predominant way that it deserves its own category.
3. **Philosophy of Life:** Giant set of beliefs about important aspects of *life*. The way you see life as a whole, people, success, money, love, society, worth, health, politics, etc.
4. **Values:** The things you give the most importance to in life, which eventually boils down to the emotional states you desire

to experience or avoid (love, success, and health vs. loneliness, failure, and sickness).

The bottom line regarding your mindset is this: *Whatever you believe to be true is the reality you'll experience in your life.* Your mindset determines who you are, what you believe and what you will do. It also determines how you organize thought, define your abilities and limitations, what you want and don't want, what is right and what is wrong, good or bad, what you can or can't do, judgment criteria, habitual emotional states and all habit patterns.

It may sound a bit overwhelming but understand that if you deal with the four key areas of Beliefs, Identity, Philosophy of Life and Values, you affect everything else in your life in a global way.

Your mindset also sets up perceptual filters to control the information that it has to deal with. At any moment, our senses are bombarded with millions of stimuli per second. Frankly, if we paid attention to all of it, we'd go nuts in no time flat. Our mindset protects us by paying attention to what's important to us, which is determined by our Beliefs, Identity, Philosophy of Life and Values.

Do you remember in the movie *Star Wars* how the Millennium Falcon would put up a force field to deflect enemy fire? It could be opened to let in friendly spacecraft but closed to keep the enemy out. In the same way, the perceptual filters notice and allow in information that agrees with our beliefs but block ideas that don't.

Unfortunately, in our mindset's automated process of protecting us, we become more entrenched in our beliefs. And if these filters block and prevent the very information that could help us change, this creates a big problem.

These filters are a projection of our mindset, of who we are. They are the lenses through which we see, hear and feel every experience and therefore determine how we interpret and give them meaning.

That's why it's possible for a group of people to observe an event and each person to have their own version of what happened. It's like the 2008 movie, *Vantage Point*, where there is an attempt on the President of the United State's life and what actually happened is pieced together as the various witnesses recount what they saw in the minutes surrounding the incident. Everyone perceived something different which made their experiences different.

These are the perceptual filters at work. They determine what you'll pay attention to, listen to and what you will believe.

It's important to know that our thoughts come from our mindset and what we are continually picking up from the thoughts others are putting out. Sometimes called the collective consciousness, ideas, concepts and beliefs held by an outside group can be very influential. We human beings are actually potent learning machines, forever trying to give meaning to things and become more aware of ourselves and the world around us.

Your mindset will vary in different areas of life based on your beliefs about that specific area. The more accurate your beliefs are (the more in line with Universal Principles), the more easily you produce desirable results in that area.

The Reality of Beliefs

A belief is nothing more than a sense of certainty about what something means. It's an idea that has so many references behind it that you feel sure it's true.

As a little boy in Cuba I loved horses. My grandfather owned a ranch and raised prize stallions. I would draw pictures of horses all the time, which my grandfather totally loved. On my fourth birthday, my grandfather gave me a white stallion. My parents dressed me up like a cowboy, complete with cowboy hat, boots and spurs. When my dad lifted me up and handed me to my grandfather on the horse, I immediately used my spurs and of course, the surprised horse started bucking. I flew through the air and, fortunately, my father caught me. They took away my spurs as punishment and I was really upset.

Over the years I've told this story many times. A couple of years ago, I was in Miami with my parents talking about Cuba and brought up the story so they could fill in some of the details that I had forgotten. They looked at me like I was talking nonsense. They asked where I got that story because it never happened and the only horse that I had ever owned was one of those toy horses with springs connected to four posts for bouncing up and down. I could have sworn my grandmother, who had passed away over 15 years ago, had told me the story when I was young. Well, they laughed hysterically insisting I imagined it and here I had been living, for over 50 years, with the reality of an experience that never happened. That is the power of beliefs (and how imagination creates them)!

The important concept to note is that a belief is *not* necessarily true. It can very easily be an absolute lie. It can go totally against the truth, but since we have the belief that it is true, our subconscious (our inner power that is working all the time to produce results) will make it true for us in our experience. Sometimes our beliefs have absolutely nothing to do with our current reality.

The truth is, there are two types of reality. The first is **Perceptual Reality**. It is what can be perceived through the senses.

The second and the real reality (pardon the pun) is **Absolute Reality**. This is Infinite Intelligence and the principles that govern everything in existence.

Perceptual Reality is where most of us live and it is nothing more than a limited view of our external world based on what we perceive with our physical senses. It is relative to what we are experiencing at any given moment in time, which means it is subject to what is happening, what we are perceiving with our senses at that moment, the emotional state we're in and the meaning we give it. It isn't necessarily true or real; *it's just our perception.* And unfortunately the foundation of the way we do this was programmed into us before we could consciously choose. It's what creates our success or failure, wealth or lack, happiness or sorrow.

For example, we live in a world where we are always accessible through various means of technology, so it's easy to perceive the worst when someone doesn't respond as quickly as we think they should. How many times have you convinced yourself that the story you created in your mind about an email that went unanswered or a call left unreturned was true, when in actuality it wasn't?

When you understand how your mind works, you realize there are two ways you can create anything: conscious (intentional) creation or unconscious (unintentional) creation. Since you are creating all the time, the question is, are you creating consciously or unconsciously? Are you creating consciously by intentionally choosing what you desire to be, do and have or unconsciously by believing that you're a victim and life is dictating to you?

Unfortunately, most people go through life allowing their attention to be pulled and distracted by others, the media and external circumstances. Our most trusted advisors, those that tell us the truth or reality of a given situation, our senses, even *our eyes*—lie to us all the time! This is because at any given time they only have one piece of the truth and it is <u>dependent on</u> other factors and variables. Even the information presented on our all-day news channels can't be taken at face value. If you've ever watched FOX, CNN or MSNBC you know what I mean.

When I talk about beliefs, I'm reminded of a story a friend told me of a Christmas dinner he attended where his wife's cousin made their family's traditional Christmas ham. When she went to serve it, her little girl asked, "Mommy, why do you always cut off the ends of the ham?"

Mommy said, "Well honey, my mother taught me to do it that way." And she turned to her mom and asked, "Why did you do it that way?"

The Grandma turned to her mother, Great Grandma, who was also there and said, "I don't know, my mother also taught me to do it that way." Great Grandma chuckled and said, "I did it that way because my oven wasn't big enough to hold the entire ham, so I had to cut the ends off!"

So everyone continued to do it that way, even though the reason behind it no longer existed!

It's amazing how many of us are limited by traditions, which are just collective beliefs, and never question them. I know people who fight and act like children when they get around their siblings at holiday time and they are now in their 40s and 50s! Or how many of you have friends that get really competitive when it comes to their favorite professional sports team? If you're within a 100-mile radius of Boston, you grow up with an infallible love for the Red Sox baseball team. If you're from anywhere in New York, you are most likely a diehard Yankees fan. But if you ask some of these fans why they love these teams, they can't really explain it; it was engrained in them from birth!

Now, the Red Sox/Yankees rivalry is a lighthearted example. But how about if you're someone who has been taught that the people in certain countries aren't worth your consideration and attention, religions that are different from yours don't require deeper understanding or even that different cultures don't deserve to be treated with respect? Worse, what if you've come to believe that *you* aren't worth your consideration and attention, understanding or being treated with respect?

You do yourself a huge disservice when you label reoccurring thoughts or repeated experiences as the one-and-only reality. If you don't question the source (sometimes the voice in your own head) and whether it's really true, you will encounter tremendous limitations.

But do not fear! The purpose of this book—and my mission—is to enlighten you and *set you free* from those limitations. There are many ways to change beliefs and I'm going to teach you powerful tools to do just that.

The Two Phases of the Mind

As I mentioned earlier, our minds are complex. While we already briefly talked about raising your overall consciousness (your mindset), increasing your awareness and being intentional in your thoughts and decisions, we now need to look at the relationship between the two phases of the mind: conscious and subconscious.

Do you ever wonder why it seems so hard to get yourself to do the things you need to do to succeed? Or why it's so hard to change a bad habit? It almost seems like there's another one of me that wants to do things their way instead of doing what I want to do, right?

This standoff is the power of your subconscious at work. We will dig further into your subconscious as we go through the book, but for now, I'd like to give you a quick overview as it sets the foundation for so much of what we're going to cover moving forward.

The *conscious mind* is the thinker. It is analytical. It is personal and selective and reasons inductively. This means that it compares all sorts of facts, data, statistics and information in order to arrive at its conclusions as to what is "true."

The *subconscious mind* is creative. It is impersonal and non-selective. It only reasons deductively, which means it never takes into account the truth or falseness of any information but **always functions on the premise that the suggestion it receives from the conscious mind or a trusted authority is correct**, and then proceeds to produce results that are congruent with the suggestion.

The conscious mind will either generate or pick up thoughts, ideas and concepts from the environment and record them on the subconscious mind. The subconscious mind receives them, like a recording device would, and then gives them form and expression, producing them in physical form in the material world. This is a Universal Law.

It's very important to understand that the subconscious mind does not originate ideas. It only accepts as true those ideas or concepts that it has been conditioned to feel and believe to be true, and then materializes them. However, once it has taken an idea or thought as truth, which we call a belief, it will continue to act on that belief with no further thought or direction from the conscious mind unless and until it is reprogrammed with a stronger belief.

The subconscious is influenced best through repetition of instruction or thought and strong feeling, whether they are positive or negative. That is why throughout this book I will repeat important concepts, ideas and instruction worded in various ways to insure your subconscious receives them. Always remember, repetition is the mother of skill.

When you don't control your feelings or you allow other people or external conditions to affect the way you feel, you impress the subconscious mind with undesirable ideas and emotional states. This is why people get confused by the results they are producing in their lives. They say, "I didn't choose to be broke or to have bad things happen to me," but by their fear, doubt, worry and listening to negative people they impressed their subconscious minds with what they didn't want to happen, and the subconscious faithfully produced it.

Look at it this way; you may have seen this picture before. Your mind is like an iceberg. A small part is above the surface of the water. The greater part of it is lurking under the surface.

Psychologists say that the conscious mind comprises 10% and the subconscious mind 90% of our mental resources. According to Bruce H. Lipton, PhD in his book, *The Biology of Belief*, the conscious mind can process 40 bits of information per second. The subconscious, however, can process over 20 *million* bits of information per second. In reality, the processing power of the subconscious is several hundred thousand times more powerful than the conscious mind because its job is to run all of the automatic processes of the body, keeping us alive and well, our organs functioning properly, the cells repairing and regenerating, etc. In addition, it takes our repetitive thoughts, particularly those accompanied by strong feeling or emotion and automates them so we don't have to think about them continually. This frees up the conscious mind to focus on new ideas and concepts and use its power of inductive reasoning to make choices.

Our subconscious mind is the powerhouse that is there to protect us, serve us and produce results. Whenever there's a mental conflict and the subconscious and the conscious are not in agreement, the subconscious wins every time because its number one priority is self-preservation.

When you try to achieve something and can't get yourself to do it or you start to succeed and as you get close you start to go backwards, what happened? *You consciously wanted to succeed but subconsciously, you had a conflicting belief that wasn't allowing it.* This is called psychological reversal. The problem is that in the process of living and learning we were infected with limiting beliefs that are causing us to self-sabotage our desires and goals.

You may say you want to be rich but your subconscious mind has a conflicting belief already programmed. Consciously you're saying, "I want to be rich," but your subconscious says, "You're full of it; I'm broke. Money is the root of all evil. All rich people are miserable and their kids are on drugs. I'd feel guilty being rich; I don't deserve to make so much money. It's hard to make money; you have to sell your soul to the devil."

Are you starting to see why it is so important to focus on expanding your consciousness, open yourself to enlightened points of view and be deliberate in all of your thoughts? It does take practice, but I assure you, you can change your mind!

To become conscious of being conscious practice catching yourself thinking. As you go throughout your day STOP and ask yourself, 'What am I thinking right now?' and simply become aware of it. As a matter of fact STOP and ask yourself that question right now.

What were you thinking?

Don't tell me you were just reading. You were also having a conversation with yourself or arguing with me or thinking about something beneath the surface of your awareness. You may have been telling me I'm full of it with all this consciousness crap, or telling yourself this is way too hard to understand. Or you may have been agreeing and thinking, 'Wow, this is really cool stuff!'

Since the subconscious mind will quiet down when you observe it, start watching it and become aware of what you're thinking all the time, because that is what is producing the reality you are living today.

For the next 24 hours, every hour (except when you're sleeping), I want you to stop and write down what you're thinking. Then go back and highlight in yellow all of the positive thoughts and use this as a litmus test for where you are currently in your thought process. If your list shines like the sun with all of your upbeat reflections, then that's fantastic, with some slight shifts you will be living your dream life in no time. If your list only has a few traces of light, don't despair. You are in the right place, with what you'll learn in this book you will get to the core of what's blocking you, break free and you will have all that you desire.

The bottom line is nothing has existence for you and me except for the consciousness we have of it. So let's keep going!

The Gate Keeper

Between the conscious and the subconscious, there is something called the critical factor. The critical factor is the gatekeeper between the conscious and the subconscious mind.

Most of us have a fully developed critical factor at around six years of age, but until then we do not have a way to filter out the truthfulness of the information presented to us. The subconscious has recorded every feeling and sensation from the moment of conception, including everything your mother felt.

Until about age six, whatever information arrived at the doorway of your subconscious mind went in unfiltered. It went in nonstop, no questioning, no rejecting what didn't make sense. It was all accepted as truth.

That is where the formation of your belief system and mindset began. Do you know people who had over-protective mothers? The little kid starts crawling around and the mother says, "Be careful, you're going to get hurt!" When he starts walking, she says, "You're going to fall. Oh, you're going to hit your head on that table! Be careful! Watch out!"

Is that child going to be confident or might that child be afraid to try new things?

For instance, if you received positive reinforcement from your parents, you found pleasure in their praise and accepted it as true. You described yourself as the smart girl or boy, gifted musician, good student, great athlete or maybe the compassionate kid who helped others.

On the other hand, say your mother had complications during pregnancy and became fearful that you would be born with health issues. She might've always seen you as a weak child, susceptible to illness, and that feeling was continually instilled in you. You assumed it to be the truth and today you may have allergies and health problems that stem from an old belief that began before you were even born.

When I was a little boy, I was very curious and was always asking questions, so my parents got me interested in books. This positive reinforcement caused me to learn to read at a very young age, a fact they celebrated repeatedly. Consequently, I became conditioned to love learning and reading, which of course helped me learn more. As a result, I did very well in school and was told that I could be anything I wanted, if I was willing to be a great student.

My first mentor was my grandfather, who had migrated from Spain to Cuba as a 15-year-old boy with just the clothes on his back. He went to work for a very successful businessman who was impressed by his humility, work ethic and willingness to learn. Eventually, my grandfather became a millionaire and the wealthy businessman's partner. As I mentioned earlier, he lost it all when Castro took over Cuba.

My grandfather taught me that the key to success lay in finding successful and wealthy people who are willing to teach you what they did to succeed. Do what they do and you'll be rich and successful, too. That advice had a profound effect on my life as you've seen thus far by my finding successful mentors to guide me while using my passion for learning to master the principles and produce great results.

What I'm saying is, we've all been conditioned. Some of it was good and some of it was not so good. Most of your belief system was being formed when you were too young to choose. You couldn't really express yourself or process information in an eloquent, verbal manner. Therefore, you have certain beliefs that are locked in as pure feelings because you couldn't describe them in words. You've been carrying around these beliefs for a long time, while being completely unaware of where some of them originated.

As parents, we don't realize all the stuff that we do to our kids. Though consciously we know better, we repeat the same patterns of our parents because of the power of our subconscious programs. I have literally asked my children to forgive me for some of the dumb things I taught them. For instance, even though in my own experience I had to overcome this belief to truly succeed in my life, I still told my older kids, "You have to sacrifice, work hard and struggle in order to get ahead!" I taught them to work at an early age and be self-sufficient which was good, but I was a bit tough on them when they complained about not liking their work. It's crazy how engrained our programming is and how often times we don't even realize it. Sorry guys! Fortunately, I did catch myself in the latter years and began teaching them that to succeed, find what you're passionate about, be diligent and master it and do it joyfully with excellence. This is the path they are all on today!

Now that you are becoming aware that *you* are in charge, you can change your mindset. In fact, you can begin reprogramming your mind on purpose and recreate yourself exactly the way you want to be, with the lifestyle you aspire to have. When you understand this truth and take control of your mind, you become master over your circumstances and start creating the life you want on purpose.

The Game Changer: Imagination

Okay, so thoughts are things.

What if you could create anything you wanted to, right now? If you're reading this on an airplane or somewhere else you'd rather not be (like maybe jury duty), how quickly can you transport yourself somewhere else? In an instant, right? You may be saying, "Carlos, I'm at the dentist's office and I've been sitting here for 20 minutes. There is no sign of that changing any time soon." Come on, think about it. When you're on the treadmill and you want to stop, what do you do to keep going? You picture yourself looking fine, strutting along the beach, right? Crossing the finish line at your first marathon. Or anywhere that is better than where you are in this moment. Whenever you are somewhere you consider unpleasant, while you may not be able to physically change your location, you can be anywhere in space and time—even the past and the future—with the use of the most incredible resource. No, not your iPad. I'm talking about your IMAGINATION.

Imagination is the creative power of Infinite Intelligence within us. It is always turned on and when directed purposely, is a driving force not to be reckoned with. I will encourage you to use your imagination countless times throughout this book, especially when I want you to abandon your standard way of thinking and really put yourself out there.

In the 1980s, Dr. Maxwell Maltz, author of the enlightening book, *Psycho-Cybernetics*, found that the mind couldn't tell the difference between a vividly imagined experience and an actual one. This is because it is the job of the imagination to create experience. Imagination is able to create anything we can think or ask, subject to the consistency of our focused attention. If we direct this power consciously by thinking from the mindset of our dreams accomplished, we will act accordingly and achieve our desires. However, if we think from a state of mind of fear, doubt and worry, we unconsciously direct this power to bring negative, unpleasant results into our lives.

You and I, in the process we call thinking, are continually having mental conversations with ourselves or others and constructing scenarios by creating mental images and circumstances and manipulating them in our minds. All of this is the function of our imagination and our imagination is functioning all of the time.

Even in our conscious mind, what we call the reasoning process, as we compare data, facts, possibilities and different points of view, we are using our imaging power in order to examine the data, view things from different angles and create scenarios while having internal dialogue. This too is imagining!

In our subconscious mind, when we remember things from our past, whether pleasant or unpleasant, the faculty we are using to recall the images, sound, and feelings stored in our memory is our imagination. When you have doubt or worry about something or when you fear something, you are using your imagination to envision or have feelings about future occurrences, conditions or circumstances. Obviously everything we envision in our future when we look at our dreams, set goals and make plans is all imagination.

The ancient teachers taught that the imagination is God in action!

Visions of beauty and splendor,
Forms of a long-lost race,
Sounds and faces and voices,
From the fourth dimension of space-
And on through the universe boundless,

Our thoughts go lightning shod-
Some call it imagination,
And others call it God.
—**Dr. George W. Carey**

The philosopher and poet, William Blake, said, "The imagination is not a state; it is the human existence itself. The eternal body of man is the imagination; that is the divine body." Blake saw imagination as nothing less than God as he operates in the human soul, as the forming or plastic spirit that works in God and in the human mind.

Albert Einstein, who is regarded as the father of modern physics, expressed his belief in the unlimited power of imagination many times stating such things as: "Logic will get you from A—Z; imagination will get you everywhere." "Imagination is more important than knowledge. Knowledge is limited. Imagination encircles the world." "Imagination is everything. It is the preview of life's coming attractions."

Einstein said that in formulating his world-changing Theory of Relativity, he imagined himself traveling through space on a beam of light. How is that for the power of imagination to change your world? Certainly by now you can see how your imagination is used in every moment in time to hold your current view of reality in place or to use on purpose to create a new reality of your own choosing.

So it is the fusion of our imagination and our mindset that shapes our world. It is the mindset from which we think that determines the objective world in which we live. In order to wisely and consciously create the circumstances you desire, the future must become the present in your imagination. Through the power of imagination, you must convert your desire into already being it and acting as if it is so. Your imagination must be centered in the state of mind of the person who has already attained your desire and view the world from that state. Our desires arise in order to be fulfilled in the activity of our imagination and what we fervently believe to be true is what will be our reality.

Chapter 4

WHY YOU BELIEVE WHAT YOU DO

Whether you believe you can do a thing or not, you are right.
—Henry Ford

Cycle of Life

I developed a model to help people better understand why we believe what we do, how our mind works and how our mindset is created. I call it the ***Cycle of Life*** because it is a self-perpetuating process that creates and reinforces the mindset that is producing whatever results we are getting.

Teaching this cycle to my network marketing organization produced such exponential growth that it surprised even my mentors. I was very fortunate to have hundreds of thousands of entrepreneurs actively participating in a laboratory of sorts, a real world setting where people were learning, testing and proving the power of these principles for over 30 years. That is why I know beyond a shadow of doubt that they work!

Mindset

Look at the visual representation of the Cycle of Life. You'll notice that the cycle begins with random experiences and external stimuli. It continues with the influence and conditioning from parents, family, friends, teachers and authority figures which produced mental associations, generalizations and gave meaning to these experiences. The result is your current mindset, which is made up of the four components we talked about earlier: Beliefs, Identity, Philosophy of Life and Values.

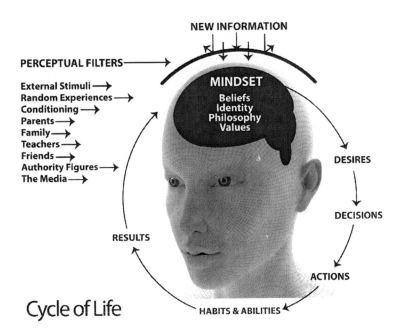

Cycle of Life

Remember that much of this conditioning took place in your life before you were old enough to make choices. You didn't <u>consciously</u> choose the conditions, circumstances or people that would influence your life before you could make decisions.

Maybe you were one of the few who were fortunate to be born into an enlightened family, whose parents had plenty of time to invest in developing a child to his/her fullest potential. However, if you're like most of us, it was hit and miss, trial and error. Moreover, today with the number of two-income families, plus single moms, having to raise their children with the influence of 1,000+ channels of TV and unlimited Internet access, who is really in control of our conditioning?

Desires

Based on your beliefs about your abilities, talents, potential for success, deservingness, worthiness and various other factors, your mindset determines your personal reality in different areas. It keeps you from desiring things it doesn't feel you deserve, aren't good enough to have, don't have the ability to do or are outside of your control. This is why some people want exotic cars, private yachts and jet planes while others think that it's decadent and even sinful to want those things.

Decisions

Your mindset with its perceptual filters also determines your decision-making patterns and criteria, how you make decisions, when and why you make them or if you make them at all. In turn, those decisions determine what actions you will take or not take on a consistent basis.

Action » Habits and Abilities

These actions (or lack of action) repeated over time will create abilities and habits, which are our automatic thinking, processing and action patterns. They will produce results automatically and these results will always be congruent with your mindset, which, by the way, validates to you that you were right all along!

Results

Your mindset determines every step along the way and produces and guarantees results that are congruent with your mindset. This is why it is so difficult to get yourself to change behaviors and beliefs. Your mind is continually validating the truthfulness of the belief by producing a result that's equivalent with the belief, thereby proving it to you.

Think about this. If I ask you, "How are you doing in life?" What would you say? Some of you may say, "I'm doing okay." "I'm getting by." "I'm *struggling* to get by." "I'm up to my eyeballs in debt." "I'm broke." But what I very rarely hear is, "I'm doing great and getting better every day!"

The bottom line is that whatever results you're producing in your life, you're doing so automatically. You're not struggling to produce the *same* results. You may be struggling to generate *better* results, but that's only <u>because you're trying to create better results while still having the same mindset that got you your current results.</u>

Let that sink in for a moment.

You were conditioned by the experiences you had before you could choose consciously. Then, you started choosing and got more results that were congruent with your mindset. All along, your mindset was being further reinforced and developed and this Cycle of Life was perpetuating itself in your life.

Breaking The Cycle

If you're not getting what you want, the question you have to ask is, 'How do I break out of that cycle? How do I escape from that seemingly endless loop?'

You break out of it by making a decision to choose new thoughts and ideas. You become aware that some of your beliefs are not serving you, so *you choose* to change them. Even though there's a cycle, once you become aware of it you can take charge of it and take control of your life.

So what do you do?

Here's what happened in my case. As I mentioned earlier, when we left Cuba, we only had the clothes on our backs, losing everything when Castro brought communism into the country. As a result, I had a lot of deep-seated fears that were conditioned in my first four years of life. My parents displayed a fear of loss that had a very powerful effect on me as an impressionable child. Add to that living in lack for several years after getting to the United States, plus the fact I didn't have a bedroom and had to sleep in a day bed in the family room until I was 13, and you have a recipe for feeling not good enough and unworthy big time. Later on, this feeling of unworthiness and fear kept me repeating strongly limiting behavior patterns.

Once I became aware of my early programming, I began working consciously to find and change my limiting beliefs. I changed all of the ones I was consciously aware of very quickly and broke my cycle. I became a millionaire and enjoyed tremendous financial success for many years. In the process I went through a painful divorce, but then met and married my soul mate and had a beautiful new baby girl. I retired at age 42 to enjoy my family and the fruits of my labor.

However, some of the fear was buried beyond my conscious memory and it's only been within the past several years that I've been able to dig deep enough to find those emotional scars. Prior to that, I thought that with the (limited) understanding of the principles I knew up to then, I could barrel through anything. What I didn't understand was I still had a lot of buried limiting fears, programs and beliefs to overcome and I would only achieve my ultimate success after I cleared those programs and broke the cycle again once and for all.

Now, I'm not suggesting that everyone has the kind of traumatic memories that I had. However, no matter what type of upbringing you had, even if you think it was perfect, there are most likely some limiting beliefs and patterns that must be addressed and dealt with so you can break free and be your best self. Otherwise you'd already have everything you want and be living your ideal life, right?

Hidden Patterns

What's your story? There is usually a pattern or story that keeps repeating itself over and over. You've got to dig up those conditioned beliefs and programs that you didn't choose and are limiting you. All of that is what's buried deep down in your subconscious and you aren't even aware of it.

According to peak performance strategist, Anthony Robbins, everything we do in our lives, we do out of our need to either avoid pain or our desire to gain pleasure.

Sometimes you get to a point in your life that's so painful that you just have to break out of it. A radical experience such as the death of a loved one, the loss of position or wealth, bankruptcy or an accident or serious illness can cause anyone to question their beliefs about who they are and what life means. You can have an "aha" experience and rise to a whole new level of awareness in a moment.

This can be seen in the story of one of my more recent mentors, high performance expert, Brendon Burchard. When he was 19 years old, Brendon suffered a tragic automobile accident resulting in a near-death experience. Following his break up with the first woman he ever loved, Brendon felt lost and like his life was over. He was so upset that he accepted a summer job opportunity in the Dominican Republic, worlds away from his home in Montana.

One fateful night, he and his friend were returning from a client's home around midnight. As they sped down the dark road through the jungle, an unmarked sharp curve drove their car off the road, flipping it through the air numerous times and crushing them in the vehicle. Bleeding and with severe injuries, they pried themselves from the car to get to safety.

Brendon survived the accident, recovered and when he talks about his experience that night, he distinctly remembers recalling the really important moments in his life and asking himself the questions, 'Did I live? Did I love? Did I really matter?' He looked up into the heavens and felt God was giving him a second chance and said to himself, 'I will earn this!' This traumatic experience served as the catalyst for his intense desire to share his story and help others to live, love and matter, which he is massively doing through his Experts Academy and High Performance Academy programs.

You don't have to endure extreme pain to have a life altering aha moment. There are other subtler ways you can create a new future.

For instance, the influence of a strong role model or caring mentor who sees your potential, takes an interest and guides you can have a profound effect and change your life dramatically, sometimes literally overnight.

Just the simple realization of the facts on these pages, facts you hadn't heard before or weren't ready to hear previously, can cause you to question your limiting beliefs and empower you to break out of the cycle.

That is precisely my point. This conditioning happens randomly in all of us until we start examining and questioning our beliefs on purpose.

Let me ask you a question.

Are your beliefs serving you and empowering you or are they debilitating you and keeping you from getting what you deserve out of life? It's time to get really honest with yourself.

Until you picked up this book, you could say that the parts of your life you didn't like were not your fault. Your mindset and all the negative ideas you'd been fed over the years were running your life. That excuse won't work any longer, because now you are learning how to take charge of your life and create what you truly desire and deserve.

Proper Use of Willpower

By now you're hopefully starting to see the importance of directing your mind on purpose to take control of your thoughts. As we have all found out at some point in our lives, willpower alone doesn't always work when we're trying to change our habits and actions. If you've ever tried to quit smoking, begin an exercise regimen, lose weight or cut out your daily Starbucks latte, you know it can be tough to do. That's because the purpose of willpower is <u>not</u> to change our actions. **The true purpose of willpower is to direct our thoughts, to focus our attention consistently, imagining our desired results achieved, which will cause a change in our actions.**

It will get the creative mechanisms of the subconscious mind and Universal Principles working for you to produce the results you desire easily, quickly and with the least effort. Pretty big reward for developing a simple habit or ability, don't you think?

Once you get down to this level of understanding of Universal Law, all of a sudden your life takes off and you just automatically start creating and producing fantastic results that will blow your mind.

The key to attracting what you desire is to focus on it continually, imagining it done, maintaining your mind in a positive state of expectancy in full faith that you have it. Assume that your desire is already fulfilled, feel that it is done, act as if it's done and you will realize it.

This is actually the most important reason to have exciting, compelling dreams and purpose-driven goals. It's much easier to maintain your thoughts on positive, constructive ideas when those ideas are so attractive and exciting to you that you want to think about them all of the time. When you focus your attention on something like that you become consumed with it and realize it faster.

Here's an example you may have experienced. Have you ever been in love and wound up with that person? It doesn't matter whether you got married or just had a relationship for a while, the key is you were madly in love and got the girl or guy.

When you met that person and fell in love, I'll bet you thought about them all the time, right? You just couldn't get them out of your mind. You contemplated being with that person, imagining all the things you'd enjoy doing together. You imagined it sparked by strong feelings so much that you produced the effect of being with that person.

I know that's the way it was with me when I met my wife, Cecy. I had just ended a 12-year relationship with a great woman who had given me three wonderful daughters that were the loves of my life, but we were just not compatible. I had purchased an apartment on the beach about five minutes away in order to be close to my girls and was not interested in starting another serious relationship.

One day, my sister, Maria, called me up and said she wanted to set me up with this incredible woman who was perfect for me. I said, "No thank you Maria, I am perfectly capable of getting my own dates, and right now I have more of them than I can handle." She was very insistent and to finally get her off of my back, I agreed, figuring I could always back out of it later.

The day of the date arrives and I'd forgotten about it and my sister calls me to make sure I'm on time. I start giving her excuses that the girls are over at my apartment and don't want to leave. She insists that I have to go and eventually I agree. Half an hour later, I call her with the same story saying I can't make it. She insists again and I eventually agree. Another half-hour later, I call Maria and repeat the process once again. This time she threatens my life and tells me she'll disown me as a brother and she'll never do anything for me ever again. At this point I figure I'd better man up and go through with it, so I take a quick shower and head down to Miami, an hour away from where I lived in Boca Raton.

Meanwhile, unbeknown to me, Maria had talked Cecy into the date as well and had offered to double date with us so she'd feel more comfortable. So when she called with my excuses, Cecy was telling her to just cancel the date since I obviously didn't want to come and frankly, she didn't want to go out either.

My sister played the whole sympathy bit, saying I was overwhelmed taking care of my three little girls and Cecy got suckered in with the adoring father/vulnerable bachelor picture that Maria painted so well.

To make a long story short, I showed up two hours late and had to double date with my sister and my brother-in-law. At the age of 37, here I was being chaperoned for the first time.

When we got to Cecy's house, my sister hurried up the walkway with me trailing behind my brother-in-law, head hanging down, hands in pockets. When the door finally swung open, I looked up and saw this gorgeous creature with the most beautiful smile I'd ever seen. I quickly straightened up, smiled and with the most romantic voice I could muster said, "Hi there, how you 'doin? Great to finally meet you!"

We went on that date sitting in the back of my sister's BMW like two giddy high school kids in love. It was love at first sight and somehow I knew that very day I had found my soul mate. I was so intent on being with her that I even delayed going to a convention in Puerto Rico the next day where I was to be the keynote speaker, just to see her again that night. I focused so much on living our lives together and really feeling how great that would be, that I "got my girl" and we've been together ever since. That is the power of compelling dreams and goals!

When you have a big dream, are you thinking joyously and with eager anticipation because you have faith a particular result is already yours and acting as if it is? Or, are you thinking intensely about wanting it and the fact that you don't have it yet, so you feel tension and anxiety?

Maybe you're out of work right now. You're checking the job boards, sending resumes, networking and doing everything you can to secure a new position. Though with each interview that goes nowhere, you become more disheartened and desperate, thinking about your future and even more urgent, your bills. Do you think that kind of energy supports or hurts your chances of acing the next interview? Now, I understand there are always other factors—the economy, the competition, pressure—we could be here all day naming them all. It can become difficult to stay focused, <u>but you must</u>. I will show you how.

The most common example that I think we can all relate to has to do with diet and exercise. Many people think about what they're giving up—the sweets and comfort food—or what they have to put themselves through—the weights, machines, treadmill and sore muscles—rather than what they're actually gaining. Instead of being in the mode of deprivation, what if you approached a new lifestyle plan with the excitement of treating your body well, increasing your energy, looking great and getting stronger every day?

The telling factor is the way you <u>feel</u> when you think about your intentions. You must get to the point where it feels good to think about your desire because you believe it's already yours and is on its way to you right now! If you feel anxiety, anger, envy, resentment or any negative energy or emotion, you are attracting the <u>opposite</u> of what you desire.

Definition of Success

People are always talking about success. How to be successful in business, have a successful relationship or marriage, succeed at losing weight/get in shape, have financial success or even successfully manage our feelings and emotions. But have you ever thought about what success actually is for YOU?

I find it ironic that so many people have never taken the time to sit down and clearly figure out what they want out of life. Those same people would never build a house without having an architect design it according to their likes and dislikes. They would spend months in the process of making changes until they got it exactly the way they wanted. But, ask them to design their own life and they look at you like you're crazy.

How would you define success? Over the past 30 years, I have found this to be a very valuable definition to start with:

Success is the progressive realization of worthwhile goals, ideals and objectives.

Let me explain it another way. We are all at a certain point in our lives today, let's call it Point A.

Now, most people are not totally satisfied where they are right now and some are downright disgusted. I'm not saying we are not grateful for the good things we have but everyone wants more, right?

So we're at point A, but where do we want to be? Lets just call it Point B.

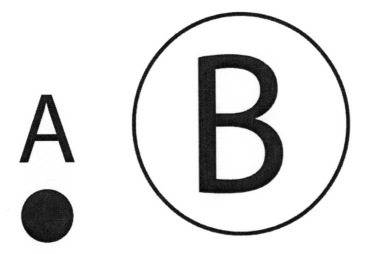

If you look at the illustration you'll see that point B is much larger because no one is dissatisfied with where they are because they have too much!

The $24 million question is: how do we get from Point A, where we are now, to Point B where we'd really like to be?

The answer is the **Ultimate Success Formula**.

In reality, anyone who has ever attained anything great in life has used this formula or a variation of it knowingly or unknowingly. It is the key to accomplishing anything in your life from material success to creating the body you desire, having fantastic relationships and finding your ideal mate. It is principle-based and produces real world results. Every time.

In order to become truly successful and achieve all the riches you want in every area of life you must:

1. ***Own Your Life.*** Take 100% responsibility for your life and everything in it. Align with your higher self and know you are worthy and deserving of all good. Discover who you really are and purposely decide who you are committed to being in this world, and create your own ideal Identity.

2. ***Design Your Life on Purpose.*** Know exactly what it is that you want. Clearly define your Point B by getting clear on your purpose in life and then defining what you desire to be, do, have and give.

3. ***Establish Your Intentions.*** Totally commit to achieving your dreams. What benefits will you and your loved ones gain by you accomplishing your objectives? Convert your desires into declarations as to who you are committed to be, do, have and give.

4. ***Discover Your Blocks.*** What has, is or could be stopping you from having what you desire? These are typically negative programs, limiting beliefs, emotional traumas, negative memories and feelings that were recorded in your subconscious early in life.

5. ***Clear and Align.*** Identify and eliminate all psychological reversal and counter intentions by releasing negative energy, memories and feelings, and transmuting limiting beliefs. Re-align with who you really are. This is an ongoing process that will liberate you the more you do it, keep you from self-sabotaging and keep you in a state of flow.

6. ***Create an Action Blueprint.*** Go to the end and see yourself already accomplishing your goals, and imagine how it feels. Figure out what you have to do to produce that end result and create a flexible plan of action.

7. **Take Inspired Action.** Take inspired action led by your inner knowing/higher self. Develop sensory acuity. If your plan isn't working, adjust according to your intuition. Stay aligned and do what you're inspired to do. Plans change, dreams don't!

8. **Be It.** Know and feel that you already are who you previously desired to be. Know and feel that you already have that which you previously desired to have. Act as if you already are, have or do that which you previously desired.

    There are two optional steps (which to me are not really optional because you'd be foolish not to use them!) that will save you time and energy:

9. **Get a Mentor.** Find someone who has already achieved what you would like in your life and learn how they think, what they believe, and how they act; then model them.

10. **Use a System.** Follow a pattern that breaks things down into chunks that you can learn and act upon more easily, and even teach to others, and you can succeed much more quickly.

When you use the Ultimate Success Formula, each powerful step in the formula works in concert with the other steps to create exponential positive results. I have broken down the steps in my system so they are easily digestible and highly effective, which you can put to work to produce positive improvement in your life immediately.

I have also included development exercises to make incremental change that will compound over time. Albert Einstein stated that the most powerful force in the universe is compounding. If you will act on these principles consistently, they will compound over time and by the end of this year your life will transform itself!

My wish is that you will take what you learn, employ it in your own life to achieve your wildest dreams and then continue to teach it to your own family, friends and community. Parents, you can teach these principles to your children now. Lead by example. Be the spouse you've always wanted to be, the daughter, son, boss, entrepreneur, innovator, philanthropist—you name it. It is all available to you. I know you're worth it and by the end of this book, you will know it—and live it—too!

Chapter 5

STEP ONE: OWN YOUR LIFE

This above all: To thine own self be true, and it must follow as the night the day, thou canst not then be false to any man.
—**William Shakespeare**

100% Responsibility for Everything!

Before you can start creating the life of your dreams you're going to have to come to the realization that you are 100% responsible for what happens to you. Your mindset has produced all of the results in your life. Whether you created them purposely by directing your thoughts to your dreams and desires or unconsciously by worrying about or fearing what you did not want. Responsibility simply means the ability to respond positively to whatever comes up.

In his classic book, *The Success Principles*, bestselling author and America's Success Coach, Jack Canfield, tells a story from a time when he was mentored by businessman and philanthropist, W. Clement Stone, and Stone confronted him with the big question, "Are you 100% responsible for your life?" Jack's answer was a bit wishy-washy and Stone told him that being 100% responsible was "the prerequisite for creating a life of success. It is only by acknowledging that you have created everything up until now that you can take charge of creating the future you want. If you realize that you have created your current conditions, then you can un-create them and recreate them at will." Jack made the decision right then and there to take 100% responsibility for his life. He then went on to cofound the bestselling *Chicken Soup for the Soul* series, which has positively affected millions of lives around the world and has also served as the springboard for the rest of his super successful career. Jack has been a very important mentor to me and I highly recommend all of his books and his Breakthrough to Success transformational seminar.

When you really think about it, being 100% responsible is actually very liberating. It puts you in control of your life. The problem is that we've been conditioned to believe that outside forces are responsible for our welfare or lack of it. We've been taught to blame others for our misfortune and lack of opportunity.

When I started out in the business world I had a victim mentality and had therefore abdicated my role as ruler of my life by giving power to other people, external situations and conditions. As I began studying Universal Principles, I started making incremental changes, little by little, taking more control over my mind and my life. Then one day, as I was studying scriptures, it all came together and I woke up. I realized I was one with Infinite Intelligence. I could do anything through this power that flowed through me and whatever I desired, if I'd contemplate, imagine, feel and act as if it was mine, would come to pass in my physical world. That day I took ownership and 100% responsibility for my life.

I signed up for that leadership seminar I mentioned, with the anticipation that major answers as to how to explode my business would be given there. Boy was I right, but not so much what I expected to hear. The secret was so much simpler and I'll tell it to you in Step Three: Establish Your Intentions.

To take full responsibility is a scary thing for many people because then they have no one to blame for their poor results or misfortune. They have given their power away to others through their belief that they are not in charge of their own lives. They have in essence made an effect their cause (remember the Principle of Cause and Effect) and the Law of Attraction is bringing them the precise results they <u>believe</u> in, thereby creating their unfortunate conditions!

The Ultimate Success Formula is a principle-based system for taking full and complete responsibility for your life, success and future! Every exercise is geared to help you gain clarity of thinking and generate the power to direct your mind and life on purpose. You must therefore give up blaming anyone, including yourself and your past, stop making excuses or looking for the cause of your failures anywhere other than your own thinking, belief system and mindset. Again, I'm not saying blame your mindset, I'm saying discover the underlying limiting belief, thought or action that is producing the negative result and take responsibility by <u>transmuting</u> it to the correct belief, thought or action that will produce the result you desire.

While none of us has yet learned how to control everything that happens to us and you will experience some frustration, especially in the beginning as you are learning to direct your thoughts purposely, you can control the meaning you give to whatever happens. You can look for the positive lessons to be learned from any adverse situation and what you learn is a benefit or gain that you can use in the future. You can choose to look at all problems as opportunities, the solution of which will bring you greater success, wealth or happiness, which is an absolute truth.

Take this as one of your foundational empowering beliefs to be 100% responsible: Nothing in life really has any meaning except for the meaning I give it. When you believe that and give empowering meaning to everything that happens, YOU truly own your life!

You really are the only one creating your life and results. You are the one who controls what goes into your mind from TV, movies and Internet content to books and magazines, to the people you associate with. Every thought, every feeling, every action is under your control. You are the only one who has the power to direct your own thinking and your mind 100% of the time. If you relinquish that right, it is 100% your responsibility to experience the results of that choice, good, bad or indifferent.

Once you've committed to take full responsibility for your life, the next step is to know who you are at a very deep level, particularly from the spiritual and mental realm.

Identity

Since the beginning of time, man has been asking, "Who am I?" and "Why am I here?" When we answer these questions and know the truth behind them, life becomes the joyous adventure it was meant to be.

One of the biggest epiphanies I've ever had was when I started learning about my identity. Up until that point I had studied about self-image but believed it was really a mask worn to show people who we want them to think we are. Identity, however, is your self-concept, who you believe you are when you're alone and naked inside your own mind.

During my personal growth in business I had undergone the natural change of identity that occurred by relating to other people's successes and in the process had become a millionaire. However, the massive transformation that took place in my life when I *consciously worked* on my identity a couple of years later was nothing short of phenomenal.

In February of 1990, I went to an amazing seminar given by Anthony Robbins, called Date with Destiny. At this time, Tony did this event at his home, the Del Mar Castle, and there were only 35 of us in attendance at this very exclusive four-day event.

This seminar was centered on creating your own destiny in life and focused on getting clear on your purpose, mission and your values. We also worked on creating a personal code of conduct. In creating this code of conduct and mission statement, my identity shifted and it became very clear to me that I could shape it any way I wanted. This was also the first time I ever wrote a purpose statement.

When I realized that by understanding who I was currently, and then deciding who I needed to be to achieve my goals, I could purposely change my own identity, it transformed my life. In the next year I increased my income over 500% and within four years I was earning 2,000% more and had one of the fastest growing marketing organizations in the world!

Your identity determines what you dare to desire, what you believe and what you'll do in your life. It defines the realm of the possible and the impossible to you and your world.

As I mentioned earlier, for most of us, our concept of who we are was created haphazardly, almost by accident, the result of random events and stimuli, past experiences and emotional states and the pain or pleasure we felt when they occurred.

In 1968, Rosenthal and Jacobson conducted the classic study, Pygmalion in the Classroom, with school children whose teachers were told that one group of children was special and would bloom intellectually and the rest of the children were average, when in fact, they were all at the same level.

At the end of several months, the *special children* exhibited greater learning capabilities and scored better on tests than the average learners. The only difference was the teacher's expectations of the children's abilities.

You and I will always act in accordance to our identity because we have an innate desire to be consistent with our self-concept. It's part of the unconscious conditioning created by those who raised us. People who are consistent are viewed as trustworthy, honest, congruent, strong, powerful, reliable, people of integrity, all very desirable characteristics that we admire. We'll do just about anything to be consistent with our identity. Even to the point of destructive behavior.

Many of our behaviors began for ridiculous reasons. Why do people start smoking, for example? Is it because cigarettes taste good? Most of us who have smoked, me included, began at a young age in order to seem older, to be cool, to be with it, to fit in. We kept smoking because it became part of our identity and even when we eventually realized the destructiveness of our behavior, we found it difficult if not impossible to quit. In my case it wasn't until I said to myself, "Hey dude, you're teaching people how to overcome their limitations and succeed in life and you're addicted to cigarettes!" that I realized this behavior was not congruent with my identity. That very day, I decided that was not who I am and haven't smoked a cigarette since!

In my years in network marketing, I witnessed thousands of identity transformations as I brought in successful entrepreneurs to share their success stories with my organizations in seminars and conventions. They spoke about their personal struggles, where they were when they started in business, and their financial, emotional and relationship challenges. Many were gut-wrenching stories, but when they told how they overcame the challenges and struggles, people related and identified and said, "*Yeah!* If they can do it, I can do it."

Let me tell you about one of these young entrepreneurs that I personally mentored. I've changed his name but this is a true story and a powerful illustration of what I'm talking about in this step.

Fred grew up in an impoverished world, abandoned by his father and mother as a very young child. He was raised in foster homes until eventually his mother reclaimed him as a teenager, but they still lived in abject poverty. If anyone ever had a reason to feel unworthiness and guilt, this kid was it. When he got involved in my marketing business he didn't own a car or even a suit, but he was hungry. He desperately wanted a way out and was willing to do anything to change.

From the very beginning he was a willing student who hung on my every word at meetings, trainings and seminars. One day we were having a big convention in Orlando and I told him he needed to be there; it was critical to his success. Since he didn't have the money to fly, he took a bus 72 hours one way just to attend! His dedication paid off as he quickly absorbed the principles and his self-concept began to transform. The change was so phenomenal it brought tears to the eyes of anyone who knew this young man previously. His identity transformation was massive and in three years he was financially free. Now he has one of the largest marketing organizations in North and South America.

The real power behind these transformations I witnessed in my business was that through this process people's identities were changing and expanding. They saw that real people like themselves, not movie stars or sports figures, but normal people, could overcome bad relationships, unhappy childhoods, poor self-images, past failures and negative conditioning and win big in life. It's a life-long process of growth because after you achieve something you once thought impossible, you begin to believe you can be more and do more, so you expand more quickly.

Anywhere in the world, the name Oprah Winfrey is synonymous with success, power and influence. She has been very open with her story and you probably already know that she came from very humble and difficult beginnings. Oprah has transformed her identity multiple times to reinvent herself, her brand and her empire. Part of her mass appeal with audiences around the globe has been her transparency about her personal journey. She has never shied away from sharing her struggles, insecurities and setbacks. She is also just as quick to reveal the clues, discoveries and strategies that have helped her and others to achieve abundance.

Her identity as a child did not restrict her from transforming her life; it fueled her passion to make her life count. In a 2007 television interview she told talk show host, Larry King, "You really can change your own reality based on the way you think." She states,

"I believe in the God force that lives inside all of us and once you tap into that you can do anything." With Oprah, there is always another level. Even today with her television network, OWN, she is paving the way with a new approach to programming, raising awareness and guiding a new generation to constantly imagine and create their best life.

Oprah is a beautiful butterfly that has chosen to keep on transforming. She keeps reinventing herself and says she's just getting started. Her story is a powerful example of the transformative power of deciding your own identity!

Discover Who You Are

If I ask you right now, "Who Are You?" how would you define yourself?

Most of the time when I ask people who they are, I'll get a blank stare or a vague statement, "I am who I am." Sometimes people will describe themselves by their occupation. I'm a doctor, a businessman or woman, an engineer, a stay-at-home mom. Others will answer based on their dominant emotions or values. I'm a loving person, I'm an intellectual or I'm a giver. Few people have taken the time to fully define and discover the beliefs they have about who they are.

To many people it's a scary thing to look inside because they know they are exhibiting behaviors they don't like. They are afraid of finding out who they really are for fear they won't like themselves. But you are not your behavior so don't be afraid to explore your current self-concept!

Take a few minutes, be honest with yourself and write your answer(s) to the question: Who are you? Understand that in discovering this, you will in no way become more bound by it. On the contrary, you can now find a way to be liberated from it.

If you're having a little trouble coming up with answers, then think about it this way, if I went to some of the people who know you best and asked them who you are, how would they describe you? The odds are those answers actually depict who you truly think you are, because we tend to project our beliefs on other people.

Write down who you <u>really</u> think you are. Don't be afraid, because it's only by knowing where you are right now that you can begin to define where you want to be and make decisions as to who you need to be in order to achieve your goals and dreams. The more honest you are with yourself, even if it's painful, the easier it will be to change. Trust me when I say a little bit of self-directed pain right now is better than the pain you'll experience for the rest of your life from not changing.

Use some of these questions to get you started.

- What is your current identity?
- What are some of the skills, abilities or characteristics that describe you?
- How would you describe yourself as a person, spouse, parent or friend?
- What level of success do you relate to your self-concept?
- Are you dissatisfied with any part of it?
- If you don't like it, has it kept you from living the life you desire?
- Has it caused you pain in the past?
- Do you think it will cause you problems in the future?
- Would you change part of it if you could?

My Current Identity[1]*

_____

_____

_____

_____

_____

_____

_____

_____

_____

_____

_____

A Future Created On Purpose

You can choose to change your identity any time you want. You don't have to choose to lose; you can choose to win. You don't have to choose average; you can choose outstanding. Your identity is your choice. Who you are now does not have to be who you were programmed to be as a child. Choose to change now.

Let me ask you this: Who do you really want to be in every area of your life?

---

1 *In my live events and online programs I do an extended version of this exercise that is very intense and creates a high level of leverage to produce immediate change. I do not include it here due to the extreme intensity of the exercise since I can't walk you through it personally. For a schedule of live events and programs go to http://carlosmarin.com/events and http://carlosmarin.com/products.

Use the questions below as inspiration so you can begin to create your future. If you feel like it, turn on music and dance if that inspires you. Do something to put yourself in a frame of mind where you feel excited so you can reinforce the life you are creating. Really think about the answers to the following questions.

- Who do you want to be spiritually?

  _____

  _____

- Who do you want to be emotionally?

  _____

  _____

- Who do you want to be physically?

  _____

  _____

- Who do you want to be financially?

  _____

  _____

- Who do you want to be as a man or a woman?

  _____

  _____

- Who do you want to be as a spouse?

  _____

  _____

- Who do you want to be as a parent?

  _____

  _____

- Who do you want to be as a friend?

  _____

  _____

- Who do you want to be as a businessperson?

  _____

  _____

- Who do you want to be for yourself?

  _____

  _____

- What do you want to do with your life?

  _____

  _____

- What is the purpose and passion that you're committed to living?

  _____

  _____

- What legacy do you want to leave behind?

  _____

  _____

Now let's take it a bit further. Imagine you have been living this new identity and life for over five years.

- How great is your life?
- How great are your relationships?
- What is your financial situation?
- How well are you doing in your career?
- What emotional states do you live in regularly?
- What kind of life have you created for yourself?
- What vacations are you taking? Where are you going? Who are you going with?

- Where are you living? What does your house look like? Where is it located?
- What do you do for fun?
- What lifestyle do you have?
- What abilities and skills do you have?
- What do you do on a daily basis?
- How have you positively affected your partner or spouse? Your children? Your important relationships? The world?
- What legacy are you creating?
- How are you living your purpose?
- How does it feel to live your passion?
- How much are you enjoying your life?

I want you to really feel those incredible emotions, the joy, the ecstasy, the passion and the success. How great do you feel? How much are you enjoying your life? What is it like?

Doesn't it feel wonderful to decide who you are and create your own destiny? Stop reading for a couple of minutes, close your eyes and see, hear and feel what it's like to be this new Super You with your new identity.

I want you to understand that if you can imagine it, you can attain it. The more you imagine it and feel yourself living that life and having that future, the easier it is to create it *automatically*.

Your assignment now is to write a statement of your <u>new</u> identity, describing exactly the person that you now are with this new, chosen identity.

Unless you have already had some success with I Am Declarations (which we'll talk about more in Step Three), you may find there's a conflict with your subconscious mind saying, 'Hey, this is BS; it's not true,' and you then find yourself psychologically reversed again. If that is the case, simply write it as, "I am *totally committed* to being…" By writing it this way you are committing yourself to <u>be</u> that person and you are lovingly suggesting to your subconscious mind to make it real.

My NEW Identity[2]*

_____

_____

_____

_____

_____

_____

_____

_____

_____

_____

_____

Read this statement every morning upon arising and every evening before you go to bed. Remember, as you keep your attention focused on that which you are committed to being, you create it and make it part of your reality.

---

2   *For an extended version of this exercise, go to http://CarlosMarin.com/usf and login to the *Ultimate Success Formula* member's area. Use your valid email address as your username and we will immediately send you a password via email which will give you unlimited access to advanced exercises, visualizations, worksheets, tools and bonuses FREE of charge! This audio file is entitled: *Your Future Created on Purpose.*

Chapter 6

STEP TWO: DESIGN YOUR LIFE ON PURPOSE

I don't dream at night, I dream all day; I dream for a living.
—**Steven Spielberg**

The second step of the Ultimate Success Formula is all about defining clearly what you desire in life. To create your ideal life, you must know exactly what you want. In other words, what is your Point B? To begin, let's dig in and expand on how you define success.

Today I personally define success as the continued expansion of happiness, knowing who I really am, living my purpose and expressing ever-greater levels of life, love and beauty. It comes about as the result of living by Universal Principles with an accurate philosophy of life that brings happiness and fulfillment.

How do we create this philosophy of life? In my experience, the best place to start is with our purpose. I believe we were all put on this earth for a reason and that reason serves the rest of humanity because we are all connected and part of the universe.

The way to find your purpose is to discover your true essence. As you learned earlier in the book, your essence is spiritual because you are an extension of Infinite Intelligence. When you know this, you know that you are unlimited pure potential and have boundless power to create what you truly desire.

Additionally, we have gifts, talents and abilities that are uniquely ours and there's at least one thing you can do better than anyone else. When you're doing this thing, you enjoy it so much that you lose track of time. You go into what's called timeless awareness.

Since the expression of your talent serves a purpose that meets the needs of the rest of humanity, you will be living your Point B, your successful, happy life, enjoying perfect self-expression.

Let me tell you the story of a young woman whose talent was nearly overshadowed by her shyness. She is another one of the students I've mentored.

Isabel was a struggling actress trying to make it in the Hispanic TV world. Although she was a very enthusiastic young lady with a beautiful, engaging smile, she lacked self-confidence, which resulted in her shyness. Her lack of confidence hampered her as an actress and certainly didn't help when she began doing network marketing. As she started learning and applying the principles of success, however, she began to blossom and believe in herself. Since she loved to perform, she found the speaker's stage to be her movie set and the attendees her fans. She had found her purpose in life.

She was so broke when she started that many times she had to take her equipment and presentation board on crowded buses to do meetings to build her business, but her dream was so big she was willing to pay almost any price. Isabel's purpose motivated her so much that she became a powerful speaker who moved audiences. As she focused on using her gifts to serve others, her confidence soared. Today she is a multi-millionaire and has built one of the largest marketing networks in the Americas.

Have you discovered your purpose yet? What did you want to be when you were growing up? Was it something you really loved to do, like dance, sing, play football or baseball, perform in some way or be an actress, dentist, or doctor? Think about it for a second.

Many people will tell you they wanted to be a lot of things but weren't good enough at any of them. However, most of us were not that disciplined when we were young, so we may not have discovered our true talents and gifts then, but we all had tendencies.

To be truly great at anything no matter how much native ability you might have, you still have to do it over and over and over to perfect your skills. The greatest basketball player in history, Michael Jordan, wasn't even a starter on his high school basketball team until his junior year! It wasn't until he committed himself to practice four to five hours a day and demand more of himself than even his coaches did that he became a superstar.

We're usually interested in certain things during our youth that are in the same general area of interest as our core purpose. We will need to hone our skills and develop the drive, discipline and vision to make the most of our gifts, but they usually are in view when we are young.

For example, when I was a kid I wanted to be a football player and the lead singer in a band. My parents strongly encouraged me to become something "worthwhile" and "respectable," preferably an attorney, since I had a facility for learning, but I really didn't want to be a lawyer. Since I lacked a dream that required an advanced education, I didn't go to college.

Eventually, I went into the insurance field, a respectable professional career. I started in property and casualty, then added life and health insurance. I was studying financial planning when I was introduced to network marketing.

I wasn't great in the insurance field because I didn't like to talk about negative things like dying, being hospitalized or car accidents. I did like working with people, however, so I focused on helping them solve their problems with insurance and as I talked about earlier, I was barely getting by and I certainly wasn't fulfilled.

On the other hand, what I liked about network marketing was that I could continually talk to people about achieving their dreams and goals. I saw myself as a business consultant who helped people improve their lives financially.

The only problem I had was a great fear of public speaking, which is no small thing in this field! I had developed this fear in the second grade in West Virginia when the other kids laughed at me because of my Cuban accent as I was giving an oral book report to the class.

I told my mentor that I didn't like to speak in public. He said I wouldn't have to do so, unless I wanted to. Finally the day came when I got tired of dragging my prospects all over town, following him to wherever he was doing business presentations. I told him I'd try doing meetings myself.

He said it was no big deal. All I had to do was make up some 3x5 cards with the information I needed to cover, tell people I was new at this and let them see how excited I was by the opportunity. He said it would all work out.

He also gave me a book called, *The Magic of Thinking Big*, by Dr. David Schwartz and pointed out the chapter on how to overcome fear. The cure for fear it turns out (and you may want to add this to your philosophy of life) was, "Action cures fear." In other words, do the thing you fear and the fear will disappear!

So I followed his advice and set out to do my first meeting. I made the 3x5 cards and even gave myself a pep talk in front of the bathroom mirror as he had suggested. I got myself all pumped up, but as I walked out of the bathroom and tried to put the 3x5 cards in my pocket, they fell onto the floor. To make matters worse, I had forgotten to number them. As I panicked, I heard the host of the meeting introduce me. I freaked out.

Seconds later, I stood in front of about 10 people, opened my mouth to speak…and nothing came out! I finally started talking but my voice cracked. I sounded like a 12-year-old kid in distress.

That night, I did a presentation that was supposed to take one hour in about seven minutes. Then, I introduced my mentor as "the person who has taught me everything I know about this business" and he finished explaining everything I had forgotten in about 55 minutes.

When he asked for questions, one guy actually said, "What do we have to do to get started? Because if that guy can do it, anybody can!"

That night, I became determined to succeed at public speaking in spite of my huge fear of rejection. It took a while but something kept driving me forward. I secretly had a deep desire to perform!

Remember, early in my life I was a performer. I was the star running back on the football team. I loved to sing and dreamed of being the lead singer in a band. The seed of the dream to be a public speaker was inside of me. I just needed to build some confidence, develop my own speaking style and acquire the right skills.

People say practice makes perfect, but it's really perfect practice makes perfect. It wasn't easy in the beginning. I'd practice my speeches and even added in some jokes and during my live talks the only person who laughed at them was me! But since I wanted it so badly, had some good mentors guiding me and great speakers to model, I began improving consistently.

I continued doing presentations day after day and after several years even got to where I practiced giving speeches in my car. Over time, with consistence and persistence, I got really good at it.

Today, if you ask me what I love to do so much that I go into timeless awareness, it's teaching people the Universal Principles of Success and doing it in public venues.

In fact, the larger the audience, the better I like it and the more fun I have. In the past 30 years, I've spoken to several million people. I've put on events where we had over 67,000 people in

ExiRed Training Event at the UNAM Soccer Stadium
in Mexico City (there are 67,000 attendees - this
picture only shows one quarter of the stadium!)

a soccer stadium for two-day business and personal development seminars.

This is my purpose in life: to teach people how to access their inner power to achieve success, happiness and wealth. I've grown a lot, both personally and financially, by pursuing my purpose. I'm on a constant journey, learning, evolving and coming into conscious oneness with my higher self. I know my purpose and am committed to use my talents to contribute to humanity.

The more I share and give, the more fulfillment and success I create in my own life. In a way, I feel like the lead singer in a band. I'm able to make people feel good and bless their lives by sharing my talents.

Finding A Passionate Purpose

> *I've come to believe that each of us has a personal calling that's as unique as a fingerprint and that the best way to succeed is to discover what you love and then find a way to offer it to others in the form of service, working hard and also allowing the energy of the universe to lead you.*
>
> **—Oprah Winfrey**

Now, let's get to the important part. What is your purpose? What are you passionate about?

The best way to go at this is to imagine God/Infinite Intelligence telling you, "I love you so much that I'm going to do something very special for you. You will never, ever have to worry about money again. I'm going to give you $50 million to start, and if you ever need more, all you have to do is snap your fingers and you'll get as much as you want."

Imagine that you already own several homes (if that's what you want!) — a beach house in the islands, in the mountains, a ranch with horses, a villa in Italy, a chalet in France, a bungalow in Fiji, a penthouse in Miami, or wherever else is your favorite location.

You also already have numerous cars — a Mercedes, BMW, Cadillac, Land Rover, Ferrari, Lamborghini, Bentley, Rolls Royce or whatever other car your heart desires.

You've taken many exotic vacations to wherever you desire, to the best beaches and the most beautiful mountains, to Europe, Africa, Asia, the Caribbean and the Pacific Islands — anywhere you've ever desired to travel.

You've helped out family and friends and given to countless charities.

Now that you have it all and you've done it all, what will you do with your life? Use the guidelines below to write a short paragraph describing how you will use your gifts and talents to serve the greater good of all.

It doesn't have to be perfect; you can refine it later. It's a work in progress that you will keep improving over the years, just as I've done mine. You will grow and change. You can't be fulfilled and happy if you don't start.

When I did my first purpose statement at the Date with Destiny event in February 1990, this is what I wrote: My purpose in life is to be the best I can be and help as many others as I can develop their full potential.

It was pretty basic but I was finding my way. That first purpose statement, as simple as it was, served me well (remember I increased my income 500% in one year) and was the basis for future growth and evolvement.

Note: Your purpose statement is not about the *how*. It's about what your life is about and makes you feel great at the very core of your being.

To be as effective as possible in writing your purpose statement:

1. Write in statements of being and doing. My purpose is to be _____ and do _____.
2. Include yourself and others. Being for yourself and doing for others.
3. State in the positive. My purpose is to <u>be</u> this and to <u>do</u> that rather than to <u>not</u> do this or to <u>not</u> be that.
4. Make it as simple and as brief as possible for maximum impact.
5. Choose something you can experience every day.
6. Do not use inflexible words such as *always, never, only,* etc.
7. Use words that carry a strong emotional charge for you.

Today my purpose statement is:

I am one with God and I am inspiring and empowering millions of people to know their inner power, be free and live their ideal life enjoying love, abundance, wholeness and perfect self-expression!

As you can see, I've evolved. You will too. Life is a journey and if you're not growing and expanding, you can never be truly happy. Start writing your purpose statement now!

My Purpose Statement

_____

_____

_____

_____

_____

_____

_____

Read this purpose statement often to make sure it moves you, that it fires something within your soul. Your purpose statement should drive you to keep growing and expanding, while also helping you recognize your connection to others and the contribution you are making.

Remember, you can refine your purpose statement any time you become aware of new distinctions or your vision becomes clearer. If you're reading it every day, you will receive insights that will help you refine it until it becomes your driving force in life. I also recommend you get the book, *The Passion Test- The Effortless Path To Discovering Your Life Purpose*, by my friends Janet Bray Attwood and Chris Attwood. It will help you to refine your purpose even more and create a new level of passion in your life.

Motive-Action!

Let's move to the second part of designing your life. Over the years, many people have told me that their main problem is getting motivated. Have you ever found yourself unmotivated and procrastinating in your work or business? I know I have and for a long time that was the story of my life. I couldn't get myself to do the things I needed to do to succeed in my business. There just wasn't any zest or excitement! But I finally understood why. My goals were too <u>small</u>.

Answer this: Can you get *really fired up* about just paying your bills or being able to eat fast-food once a week? Can you get totally pumped and excited about just getting by, feeling so-so or being average?

Before anyone feels insulted, remember that you are unlimited potential and Infinite Intelligence doesn't create average; It doesn't make junk. It's people who choose average. If you want to overcome average and be excited and motivated on a continual basis, you have to think big; you have to think of the possibilities.

To have tremendous motivation, you have to have tremendous goals that drive and compel you. It's time to let go of your fears and preconceived notions. You see, motivation is really a <u>motive</u> that is so compelling that it drives you to take <u>action</u>. It is **motive-action!** The big question is where do we find such a big motive? The answer, like most things in life, it's already inside of you. You don't actually find it; **you define it.**

My friend, Marcia Wieder, founder and CEO of Dream University and best selling author of *Making Your Dreams Come True,* teaches that everything is possible even if you don't know in advance how you're going to achieve it. The key to happiness is to have a big dream that brings you more joy and fulfillment, more passion and energy. She states that getting your dreams out of your head is critical yet for many it's the hardest step. A dream is simply something that you desire, but since our minds are filled with reasons why we don't believe we can have them, talking about them and writing them down is the first step towards achieving them. If you want to get super clear on your dreams she has excellent programs that can show you how.

So let's do a powerful exercise that I've taught people for many years to define and get total clarity on what YOU truly desire. The rules of this exercise are simple: don't prejudge if it's possible or probable and simply let your imagination go wild like it did when you were a kid.

I'd like you to imagine that you can be, do, have and give anything you desire in life. Anything at all, what will it be? Use the pages in the book or you can get out four sheets of paper right now and label each page in the following succession: Be, Do, Have, Give.

As you prepare to do this exercise, imagine once again Infinite Intelligence telling you that It's going to grant you all the desires of your heart in the key areas of your life (BE, DO, HAVE, GIVE) that you can write down in five minutes.

This is brainstorming. Have you ever brainstormed anything? You don't hesitate, over-think or rationalize. You don't start thinking, is 6,000 square feet too big? Should it be only 4,863 square feet? Is a Bentley too gaudy? Should I just settle for a Toyota? What will people think of me if I have my own airplane? Is it too decadent? What about my own chef? What about desiring a soul mate that is drop dead gorgeous, loving, giving, and… am I asking too much?

Don't second-guess yourself. If you've ever thought about it in your wildest dreams, write it down. If you wanted it when you were a kid, write it down. Before you learned to feel guilty about having money and riches, did you think about having it? Before you became a dutiful, decent, self-sacrificing human being, did you think about having it?

Be-Do-Have-Give

Let's start with BE since it has been the focus of the first two chapters. This is a really powerful area that massively impacts your life. We've worked on identity and purpose, but doing this exercise in this format actually helps to expand it.

Before you start, take a deep breath and really imagine God has given you the ability to make all your dreams come true. You have been transformed into the person you know is inside you, the person you've always desired to be. You can even close your eyes for a few moments to really picture it.

Write everything you even remotely think you might want to BE in your entire lifetime.

By the way, that doesn't just mean I want to be a millionaire, billionaire or gazillionaire. It's I want to be a loving father or mother, a great friend, a phenomenal speaker, the man/woman who changes the world, a best selling author, a famous musician, a philanthropist, an artist or financially free. So go for it now!

BE

_____

_____

_____

_____

_____

_____

_____

_____

_____

_____

_____

_____

_____

_____

_____

_____

_____

_____

_____

_____

_____

_____

_____

_____

Now, write down everything you think you may want to DO.

Again don't prejudge. Don't disqualify yourself. Remember, God is giving you everything you can write down in the next five minutes because He loves you so much and you're such a great person. I'm serious, don't let the guilt get to you. Today, be that little kid; you can always go back to being an adult later. It's time to let yourself go.

Let your imagination go wild! Again, pull out all the stops. You can do anything you want. Maybe you want to...

- Climb Mount Everest.
- Sail around the world in a sailboat.

- Spend a couple of months in Tahiti.
- Create a foundation for kids.
- Take six months and work on yourself spiritually.
- Build a huge business.
- Learn how to fly, sky dive, play the guitar or write a book.
- Produce your own movie or TV show.

What do you want to do? Remember, this includes anything and everything, from playing sports or musical instruments to hobbies, cultural interests and accomplishments in business.

DO

_____

_____

_____

_____

_____

_____

_____

_____

_____

_____

_____

_____

_____

_____

_____

_____

_____

_____

_____

_____

_____

By the way, some of these things are interchangeable and wind up in multiple categories. For example, in the BE category, you may say, "I want to be a millionaire." In the DO area you may say, "I want to build a multi-million dollar business." In the HAVE part you may say, "I want to have $1 million or $5 million." These are all valid, based upon the way you process information.

Let's move on to HAVE. For many people this is the easiest area because it's all about the *stuff*. It could be any material thing from houses and cars to jewelry, boats, expensive toys, to businesses, income, relationships, finding your soul mate or having your ideal body or anything that you can physically obtain, whatever falls into the category of HAVE.

Remember, don't prejudge at all. You can always do that later. Let your imagination go wild and even if you're not sure that you desire it, if it pops into your mind, write it down. You can always take it off the list. Don't miss out on something that you may truly desire by second-guessing yourself.

HAVE

_____

_____

_____

_____

_____

_____

_____

_____

_____

_____

_____

_____

_____

_____

_____

_____

_____

_____

_____

_____

_____

_____

_____

Last but not least, write down everything you want to GIVE or contribute.

For many people, this can be the most compelling goal because here is where you make a contribution to mankind and leave your mark on this world.

Write down everything you'd like to share or GIVE, any type of contribution at all, whether it's money or time or building an organization that impacts mankind, such as:

- Contribute to your church, synagogue, temple or favorite religious organization.
- Create a foundation to feed and clothe underprivileged kids.
- Help save the rainforest or even a local landmark.
- Give time to a group that protects battered women or at-risk youth.
- Work pro bono for an organization that needs support in your specialized field.
- Volunteer in your child's school.
- Become a mentor.
- Advocate for patients' rights.
- Organize and plant a community garden.
- Donate to find a cure for cancer.
- Host a gala for your favorite charity.
- This list goes on…

But don't stop there. Also consider what you'd like to give your spouse, children, parents, your friends or anyone else you care about.

GIVE

_____

_____

_____

_____

_____

_____

_____

_____

_____

_____

Wasn't that fun? Are you excited? So now, go through the list of desires you've written and determine when you truly want to achieve or realize each one. As you go through them, if you find that you wrote something you don't really desire, just scratch it out. Alternatively, if your juices got flowing by doing these exercises and you realize you've sold yourself short, you can increase the size of any of these desires.

As you go through the list, put the number 1, 2, 5 or 10 beside each item, indicating the time frame in years in which you're committed to having it.

Put the number 1 beside the ones you're committed to achieving in one year or less. Put a 2 beside those you're committed to achieving in two years. Put a 5 beside those you're committed to achieving in five years. Put a 10 beside those you're committed to achieving in 10 years or more.

Please understand, this is not an exam; this is a gut check. This is not a head thing; it's not something you're reasoning out and analyzing. There are no right or wrong answers, except what you feel to be right. Your inner knowing will tell you by how you're feeling. Take a few minutes to do this now.

Vision Board

If you want to take this process a step further, I suggest you make a vision board. You may have heard this a few years back in the movie, *The Secret*, but I was doing this and producing fantastic results with it long before this concept became so well known in pop culture.

Go find pictures in magazines and on the Internet that represent all those things you desire. The houses, cars, jewelry, planes, yachts, vacations! Find a body in a magazine you'd like to have and put your face on it.

If you want a soul mate, describe him or her and find a picture of someone whose looks you like, put your picture beside it and then put your description of the type of person you desire to be with under the picture.

If you want a certain business, position or title, or success in a certain area, find a picture that's representative of it and put a picture of yourself in it as the central figure. Want massive wealth? Get a picture that represents wealth and tie it into yourself or your life graphically in a way that means something significant to you.

Have fun with it! Remember, by having the pictures in front of you, you will imagine what you desire more easily. And believe me, I know how this works in a massive way from personal experience.

Years ago, my office manager gave me a gift for my birthday. It was a poster of the back of a beautiful mansion, with a boat docked behind it and a BMW and a helicopter parked on the lawn.

The heading on it read, "ALL I WANT IS WORLD PEACE AND…" Well, I thought it was the coolest thing so I framed it and put it in the library in my house in Atlanta where I could see it from my desk every day.

A few years later I decided I didn't like the winters in Georgia so I moved back to Boca Raton, Florida. I bought this spectacular home on 2.5 acres on the Intracoastal. One day we were shooting a lifestyle video for an event we were having and my production guy wanted to shoot footage of me going down the Intracoastal in my yacht, right behind my house.

When I saw the finished video I freaked out because he had taken a shot of my poster and then faded into the live video he shot of me in my yacht behind my house and they looked almost indistinguishable.

I had bought a house that was virtually identical to the poster I'd had hanging on my wall for three years without even thinking about it consciously. But the most powerful thing was I could've never afforded that house when I got the poster. My income increased 1,000% (that's 10 times the income) in those three years, which is what made it possible for me to buy it. Wow!

I highly recommend you create your own vision board and watch what results you'll produce. It works!

Chapter 7

STEP THREE: ESTABLISH YOUR INTENTIONS

Once a man has made a commitment to a way of life, he puts the greatest strength in the world behind him. It's something we call heart power. Once a man has made this commitment, nothing will stop him short of success.

—**Vince Lombardi**

No Such Thing as TRY

Let's talk about a topic that concentrates and animates your power to create whatever you want in your life. That is the power of commitment. Commitments are irreversible decisions that convert wishes and desires into total intent backed by action.

The life you are living today is the result of the decisions you made in the past. The life you'll have in the future will be the result of the decisions you make today. That's powerful stuff!

Okay, another *Star Wars* reference. Can you tell I'm a huge fan? In *The Empire Strikes Back*, Luke Skywalker goes back to see Yoda to finish his training to become a Jedi Knight. When he enters the atmosphere of the planet Yoda is living on, he loses control of his ship and crash-lands his starfighter into a swamp. Yoda appears and tells him to concentrate the full force of his attention and will it (intend it) to come out of the swamp. Luke closes his eyes and concentrates and the starfighter starts rising up out of the water. Then he loses control and the ship falls back into the swamp.

Yoda tells him to concentrate harder and make the ship rise out of the swamp, but Luke doesn't believe it is possible. Just as he is about to give up, Yoda implores him once more. Luke replies, "Alright, I'll give it a try," to which Yoda quickly responds, "No! Try not. **Do or do not.** There is no try."

Think about it a moment; this is a very deep message Yoda is giving Luke. It's also a huge message for you and me! What does this mean, there is only do or <u>do not</u>? In Yoda's reverse-speech, it means you either do it or do not do it. Where does do or not do come from?

As you're reading this, I hope you've been participating in the exercises, so you probably have a pen close to you. I want you to lay the pen down in front of you. Now, "try" to pick up your pen. You might be laughing saying, "What do you mean <u>try</u>? I'll pick it up if I want to or not pick it up if I don't want to."

Do or not do is a decision you make. Obviously, it's a simple decision with something easy like picking up your pen. What happens if I tell you to pick up your pen and write a 20-page report on quantum physics?

Do or not do becomes a function of your belief in your ability to write the report. It's also a reflection of how much knowledge you have about the topic, which is obviously a reference that causes you to have or not have belief in your ability to write it.

There's also your desire to write the report. If you wanted to do it badly enough, if there was a big enough reason or reward for you to do it, you would get a book on quantum physics, read it and write the report. The point is that in our culture today, **we use the word try as an escape route from the absolute total commitment implied in making a true decision.**

Luke didn't believe in his ability to lift the starfighter out of the swamp with the power of his mind. So he *tried*, which means, "I'll do it if I can without total commitment."

Of course, the power of commitment does not just belong on screen. I'll share the story of another one of the people I've mentored to show you how it works in real life.

Juan had defected from communist Cuba when his plane stopped for fuel in a neutral European country, where he wound up staying for several years. He eventually migrated to the US and was working as a truck driver earning $15,000 per year when I met him. He was a bright 25-year-old kid but it was evident that, although he'd wanted to escape the tentacles of communism, its strongly conditioned programming was deeply engrained in his character. It was obvious, because he was always looking to beat the system and circumvent the rules.

It took quite some time to gain his trust and even longer for him to start changing his belief system. He was suspicious of everything. His entire belief structure had been built on a faulty foundation that was dependent on a philosophy of manipulation. As I helped him build his *business and he saw me achieve massive success, he started to develop a big dream of his own. When he <u>totally committed</u> to his dream, he began to believe in himself and he became unstoppable. His limiting programs began to give way to an empowering new mindset and his progress was so fast it was amazing to watch. He became a dynamic public speaker and leader and within five years had built a huge business that generated a seven figure per year income.*

De Caedere

What does the word *decision* mean? It comes from the Latin root "De Caedere" which means to cut away from completely. When you make a decision, you literally cut away from any and all other options or alternatives. Today we would actually call it a commitment, because people change their decisions almost like they change their underwear.

When was the last time you made one of those De Caedere commitments?

Typically, when we say, "I made a decision," we mean, "I'll do it if it's easy. I'll do it if it's comfortable. I'll do it if I don't get flack from other people. I'll do it if results come quickly. I'll do it if I have the time."

To truly succeed in any area of life, our decisions have to mean, "I'll do it no matter what!"

In 1519, there was a Spanish captain named Hernán Cortés who lead an expedition to Mexico, to expand colonization in the area of Veracruz. When his fleet reached the shores of the mainland, they encountered severe resistance and enemy combat. Cortés, in an act of solidarity with his men, ordered them to burn their own boats. As the ships were going up in flames, the message was clear that there was no turning back. It was either win or die right there.

What do you think happened? They won! The power of his commitment is what determined their success in the battlefield. This is what a true decision is all about — getting totally committed, cutting off all sources of retreat. Cutting away from any and all other alternatives is the only way to guarantee success and victory in any undertaking.

When a true decision is made, action is its natural consequence. In the commitment, the action is birthed. When you create the habit of making true decisions, you begin to have faith in your decisions because each is a total commitment. Then you know, beyond a shadow of a doubt, that the result is around the corner.

As I mentioned previously, in my first business I struggled for the first three and-a-half years as I was learning the principles of success and changing my mindset. One of my mentors, former professional football player, Tim Foley, was totally frustrated with me and continually told me that I had much more potential than I was demonstrating. He said I was too distracted with my energy business and lacked commitment. Then I watched his business grow tremendously over the course of a year as his persistent efforts came to fruition. When he told me how much he was making I realized his income tripled mine while he only worked a third of the hours that I did. I figured one of us was stupid and it wasn't him.

It was during this time that I had the awakening I previously shared with you and made the decision to go to that leadership seminar which changed my life. I heard that speaker who had achieved his goal of becoming a millionaire in two-and-a-half years say that the reason most people attending the seminar were not where they wanted to be was they hadn't "sold out" to their business. They were walking around like they had so many other options but the truth was most people had no other options that could even come close to providing the income, wealth and lifestyle of a millionaire in his business. He said that the key to becoming wealthy was <u>total commitment</u> to your dream and massive, consistent action to achieve it.

He explained that when he started he was on the verge of bankruptcy in his construction business and had a big dream to be wealthy. When he looked at his mentors he didn't feel he was as sharp as they were but he knew he could outwork anybody. He took the level of activity that was being taught to build a successful business and doubled it and committed to do it until he became a millionaire. So that's exactly what he did.

I had a second awakening and realized right there that this was my problem. I had been afraid to fully commit due to fear of failing and rejection, so I kept dabbling in other businesses. Up until then, I hadn't made a real De Caedere decision to go for it. I hadn't burned my bridges and cut away from all other options. I was negotiating the price for success and had negotiated it to a higher price. I made that true decision right then and there that I was going to do the exact same thing and outwork everybody, which ironically is exactly what I had done to excel in sports growing up.

When you make a De Caedere decision, you know that all you have to do is put in the proper amount of action and you'll get the results. The key is the commitment. You can change your entire life in one moment with the power of a true decision. As a matter of fact, you'll never put forth the action required without first making a real decision.

There's a verse in the Bible that says, "Faith is the substance of things hoped for, the evidence of things yet unseen" (Heb. 11:1). Faith is total belief and conviction that something that is not seen is real. Commitment is what unlocks the door to mountain-moving faith.

When you really learn how to make De Caedere decisions, they become a thing of power and in the decision the goal is already achieved because it is that level of commitment that turns desires into full-blown intentions.

All of a sudden, you begin to attract the people and circumstances needed to achieve the result you want. You begin to see the opportunity in problems and realize that they were things you needed in order to achieve your goal.

Decision is the partner of focus. Decision is intention and focus is attention. As bestselling author and physician, Deepak Chopra, states in his book, *The Seven Spiritual Laws of Success*, the two qualities inherent in consciousness are attention and intention. Attention energizes and intention transforms.

When you decide something, since you have cut away from all other alternatives, you totally and unequivocally intend to make this a reality in your life. Since your intention is to create what you decided, you maintain your attention on it. The natural question you continually ask yourself is, 'What do I need to do now in order to move closer to my intended outcome?'

When you focus on your dream and decide that it will be your reality, you will live and act on it as if it is already your reality and you will achieve whatever you want in life.

I Am Declarations

Let's look at the exercise we did in the last chapter. You should be pretty darn motivated right now because you are truly starting to design your life on purpose. With what you've just learned on the power of decision and commitment, you are in a position to turn those desires into intentions and set them in the fertile field of consciousness to turn them into physical reality right now.

Look at the four lists you created in Chapter 6: Be, Do, Have and Give. Pick out your top three two-to-five-year dreams from each list. In each category, these should be the top three goals that would transform your life in the next two to five years once you attain them. They should be the top things that totally motivate you, fire you up and get you excited about your life. You are now going to write them in the space provided as **positive, present-day declarations written in the first person, I am, I do, I have, I give.** I call these first person, present-tense statements, I Am Declarations for short, because I Am is the undifferentiated potential of Infinite Intelligence, which is within all of us. Whatever you declare afterwards is the reality you are ordering into existence so it also applies to I have, I do and I give!

This is why you're <u>not</u> going to write your declarations stating: I *will* be that, do that, have that or give that, because then that would always keep these things two to five years in the future. You are going to make a De Caedere decision, a total commitment to being, having, doing and giving these things today.

The purpose of this exercise centers on the Law of Belief, which shows that we continually have mental and vocal conversations about what we believe to be true, which directs what we focus on and attract into our lives. It isn't only what you focus on continually, it's the vibration that you're putting out to the universe based upon what you believe is yours. This is the meaning of the scripture, "Whatever you desire when you pray, believe that you receive it and you shall have it" (Mark 11:24). Furthermore, what you speak out loud carries increased vibrational power that influences your actions to create physical realities. That is why the scriptures also state, "By your words you shall be justified and by your words you shall be condemned"

(Matt. 12:37) and "Death and life are in the power of the tongue" (Prov. 18:21).

By affirming these I Am Declarations you are using the power of your words to direct your thoughts and mind positively and purposely, creating and reinforcing a new empowering belief that will get you what you want. Then as you're focusing on whatever the ideal outcome is for you, here's what happens. You imagine the ideal picture of your life as it will be in a couple of years and focus on it continually, morning, noon and night with total belief and expectancy that it's already yours. If you had already achieved all of those things, wouldn't you be excited? Of course you would, so this is creating a mental attitude of success, positive expectancy, appreciation, gratitude, happiness and confidence, which is the vibration you are sending out into the world. Like attracts like, so by the Law of Attraction, this is what you are drawing to yourself <u>automatically</u>.

For every category, Be, Do, Have and Give, take the top three two-to-five-year intentions and write them in the present tense. As you rewrite them you may want to make them even more specific, so you can really focus your attention to exactly what you desire.

For example:

BE Goal: Be a millionaire.
Declaration: I am a millionaire.
DO Goal: Open my own business.
Declaration: I own a highly successful business.
HAVE Goal: Build a toned and fit body.
Declaration: I have my ideal body. I am toned and fit.
GIVE Goal: Give annually to my favorite charity.
Declaration: I give $20,000 annually to my favorite charity.

Once I got totally committed to my goals, I created some very powerful I Am Declarations that I repeated many times each day in order to direct my focus, create empowering beliefs, live in positive emotional states and reprogram my mindset. Here are what mine were back then so you can have a better example:

- I am a multi-millionaire!
- I own a $20 million dollar business.
- I am earning over $1,000,000 per year.
- I have the fastest growing marketing organization in the world.
- I am giving over $100,000 per year to my favorite charities.
- I have my ideal body. I am muscular, super-fit and at my ideal weight.
- I have perfect health, tremendous energy, vibrancy and vitality.
- I have a loving, romantic, and fun relationship with my soul mate.
- I have loving, fun and influential relationships with my kids.
- I am a state master. I direct my focus and emotions continually.
- I am a man of mountain-moving faith and a massive action machine.

See? It's pretty basic, but the impact of writing, feeling and visualizing yourself as if you have it is extremely powerful.

What are you waiting for? Get writing and enjoy the process!

My I Am Declarations

I AM

1. _____

2. _____

3. _____

I DO

1. _____
2. _____
3. _____

I HAVE

1. _____
2. _____
3. _____

I GIVE

1. _____
2. _____
3. _____

You now have the foundation to change your life by being clear on what really moves you, drives you and inspires you to go to new heights of awareness. You are creating new empowering beliefs and thought patterns through the use of your I Am Declarations. You use your imagination to see and feel as if you already are, do, have and give this, and then use it as a lever to transform yourself and automatically produce what you desire.

If you don't like your current results, could it possibly be that you didn't specifically decide what results you truly wanted, or that you didn't set your sights high enough to really get excited about them? And, if you didn't clearly ask life for what you wanted and additionally sent life mixed signals… how could you get what you desired?

This exercise is the catalyst to get you where you want to go automatically. Your assignment is to read and state your I Am Declarations first thing in the morning when you wake up and imagine yourself as already being that person, doing and having your desires and giving value to the world. Also read and declare them before you go to sleep at night and declare them as often as you can during the day to further cement them in your mind.

Please remember that just reading all of this will not create the changes you want in your future. You must put these principles to work in your life! Apply these strategies, state your I Am Declarations often and take massive action; do what you've never done before.

By the time you're done with this book, you are going to know how to direct and focus your mind and manifest your desires on purpose, automatically!

Chapter 8

STEP FOUR: DISCOVER YOUR BLOCKS

That which does not kill us, makes us stronger.
—Friedrich Nietzsche

Thoughts Become Beliefs

While I've always been a big proponent of turning desires into burning intentions and focusing on their attainment until they become physical realities, it is important to understand that we have limiting beliefs and programs running in the background of our subconscious mind that often block their achievement. Let's quickly review beliefs to put this concept back into perspective.

We continually process ideas and concepts that have been presented to us and contemplate them in order to understand them, categorize them and give them meaning. This is called thinking. A persistent thought, over time, develops a sense of truthfulness about it and becomes a belief. Once a thought is a belief, it goes into the automatic mode in our subconscious mind and we don't have to think about it any more. From here on, it will shape how we view things and mold our life experience.

Since ideas are the basis of thinking, where did we get them? We got them from everything we've seen, heard and experienced from the time we were born. All of these ideas are stored in our subconscious mind and then, based on our thought patterns, they pop up, either continually or from time to time.

The thoughts and beliefs that keep playing over and over in our minds that result in behavior or habits that we cannot change are simply subconscious programs that were conditioned in us earlier in our lives.

As you learned in Cycle of Life, we all have had well-meaning people in our lives that have tried to protect, teach and guide us. Remember, they couldn't give us what they didn't have and they didn't know what they didn't know. In our early years our critical factor was not yet fully developed so we couldn't reject their influence. They were doing the very best they could, according to their level of awareness. However, that doesn't change the fact that during that process we may have had experiences resulting in painful emotional scars and traumas which produced limiting beliefs and negative programs that keep us from having the results we desire.

My Perspective on Limiting Beliefs

Throughout my years of teaching the principles of the Ultimate Success Formula live, on stage, I've gotten used to certain terminology for distinctions and processes. Writing this book and putting everything down on paper caused me to reevaluate and question my word choices and language. I especially went back and forth with Cecy and my editor about the word limiting when it comes to negative beliefs. Was limiting the right word? Had I been using it for so long, unconsciously, that I was missing a more suitable description? After lengthy discussions, I found myself passionately defending this word and here is why. Limiting is a self-imposed or a belief-imposed boundary that inhibits us from being able to utilize the power that we have within us. It is a catchall phrase because some beliefs that hold us back are inhibiting, but then others are debilitating. Some are restricting, being forced on us by outside sources. There are binding beliefs and others that are conflicting, always in battle. Some beliefs are damaging and yet others are downright devastating. Any way you slice or dice it, all of these beliefs limit you from accessing your personal power to achieve whatever it is you want.

As you know, my own life offers a good example of what I'm talking about. I've shared it with you so you can see how negative programming comes about and understand how important it is to overcome it. I have experienced loss in my life because I was conditioned and unconsciously trained to expect it. I had attained all of my success in business by totally focusing my attention on my dreams, imagining it being so and excluding everything else from my view. But, as I attained more and more financial success, I began to feel an emptiness inside, which prompted me to seriously start questioning if what I was doing was fulfilling my true purpose in life. As I became more dissatisfied, since I didn't yet understand some of the concepts I'm teaching you here, I allowed myself to focus on what was wrong with the situation, once again using the old familiar fear of loss to motivate myself as I had done in the past.

In hindsight, it is evident to me that I didn't understand how much buried fear I had. Knowing what I know today, I realize that a series of events triggered these deeply covered fears. Drastic political and governmental changes in various countries affecting my global businesses activated my fear of loss while at the same time fear-based advisors were influencing me to make bad business decisions thereby compounding the problem.

The fear of loss engrained in me during my formative years was sparked and blended with my current fears, creating a financial whirlwind in my life. Ironically, I used the very same power I'd used to create success and wealth (the consistency and intensity of my focus), except now in reverse (imagining what I didn't want to happen), and the fears that were hidden deep in my subconscious mind attracted what I was fearful of into my life.

Remember that thoughts, beliefs and emotions are the cause of all experiences and conditions, even if they are buried in your subconscious. This is how the Law of Cause and Effect works every time. However, once I realized I had this unconscious limiting program it started me on a whole new path of learning, and transmuting those programs has produced an exponentially higher level of consciousness and power in my life.

Back in Step One (Chapter 5), I asked a simple question: Who are you? For me, knowing my true identity at that point in my life empowered me to believe that I could be successful again but I had to get really clear so that I could release all of my negative programming and once again re-design my life on purpose. The level of true-place success, self-expression, love, wealth, wholeness, joy and happiness I enjoy today was more than worth the small price I paid!

You must discover what it is that's holding you back. Don't suppress or go into denial. If you're not demonstrating riches, you have some subconscious limiting beliefs. We all have them and we just need to discover what they are, so we can replace them with empowering beliefs.

It's on the Way to Me Right Now

Your beliefs not only represent what reality is to you but they continue to manifest current and future realities in your life.

When bad things happen, we resist the idea that we have attracted them into our lives. It's not that we want to attract the bad stuff, it's that we have conflicting beliefs that we are unaware of that are creating resistance and that is what attracts it. Until we clear the conflict, which is why you'll hear me talk about clearing, your subconscious does not have precise instructions and will continue to produce results based on the old unconscious belief.

Psychologists sometimes call this being psychologically reversed, which simply means you have conflicting desires or beliefs. Your conscious mind wants one thing while your subconscious has been conditioned to produce the opposite. As we've already seen, when this occurs, who wins the battle? The subconscious wins 100% of the time!

Let's take a couple of examples so you fully understand.

We'll start with the obvious one: I want to make more money, or better yet, I want to be rich. Consciously you believe this, you really think it's your goal and may have set it as a goal many, many times. You may have even created a plan of action for its attainment, gotten into a new business and set off after the goal. Along the way, you may have experienced a little bit of success, but somewhere along the line you reach a point that you can't seem to get beyond no matter how hard you try. Then you beat yourself up and might say, "I knew it was too good to be true," or "Why do these things always happen to me?" or "Why does it seem I can't get ahead?" This is called self-sabotage and is just another word for psychological reversal.

If something like this has happened to you, you have some underlying beliefs that prevent you from achieving the success or wealth that you desire. It may be that you heard money is the root of all evil from the time you were very young. You may have heard family members say that rich people are miserable. You may have heard them say love is more important than money, presupposing you can only have one or the other. You may have heard things like you have to be brilliant to be rich or you have to sacrifice family and fun.

I am sure you get the picture and by now you can probably add a whole series of things that you heard from family, relatives, parents, religious leaders, teachers, coaches and many other sources.

Another example many people can relate to is the desire to lose weight. Again, you may have set a goal or made a New Year's resolution many, many times to lose those unwanted 15 to 20 pounds, which may have turned into 30, 40 or 50 by now. Consciously you want to lose the weight, but unconsciously there is a belief or a series of beliefs that are keeping you from achieving your objective. It may be that as a child you were told to make sure you cleaned your plate because there's a lot of hungry people all over the world with nothing to eat (did this ever make sense?). Perhaps as you were growing up, whenever you felt bad or had a problem, one of your programmers, I mean teachers, would give you some chocolate, candy, cookies or ice-cream to cheer you up and make you feel better. So that not only created a sugar addiction, but also developed a pattern that whenever you felt badly, some sweets made you feel better.

It can be as complex as being in a relationship with somebody you really thought you loved and being terribly hurt when they left you. You gained weight from any combination of beliefs from the past, including, 'eating makes me feel better.' As you got heavier, your subconscious began using the extra pounds as a protective mechanism to keep members of the opposite sex away. Now every time you try to lose the weight, your subconscious says, 'Oh no, you are forgetting that time we got really hurt.' Consequently, it keeps you from losing the weight you desire to lose in order to protect you.

This is what resistance is and it can happen in any area of your life. You may ask, "How do I know if I have resistance?" And my reply to you is, "Is there anything you desire in your life that you currently don't have?" To which you would obviously answer, "Of course." Then I would say, "Well, why don't you have it?"

Unless your answer is, "It's on its way to me right now," and you say it with absolute certainty, you have resistance. Any time that you don't have what you desire in your life, you can be sure that you have resistance. You have conflicting beliefs and you must release the resistance and get clear.

Define YOUR Limiting Beliefs

What limiting beliefs do you have that you need to change in order to achieve what you want out of life?

The key to changing limiting beliefs is to understand that *your beliefs must be congruent with your desires* or you will be psychologically reversed and self-sabotage. The first few steps of the Ultimate Success Formula begin with the end in mind, by immediately defining clearly your most compelling desires. All of the changes you need to make in your life and the motivation you need to make them are contained in the dreams and intentions you have already defined.

Just as your identity must be congruent with what you desire, your belief system also needs to be congruent with your desires in order to achieve them. To have Point B results you must think, believe and act like a Point B type person.

What beliefs do you need to change now in order to be congruent with your desires and dreams?

Maybe it's something like:

1. I'm too old or too young.
2. I don't have enough education/the right education.
3. I don't deserve success because of my past mistakes.
4. People are against me/are out to get me.
5. I'm black, Hispanic, white (I don't have the right ethnic background).
6. I don't have time.
7. The economy is so bad that you can't make money today.
8. You have to have money to make money.
9. My duties as a mother/father (whatever) limit me or my spouse doesn't support me.
10. I don't have the right skills.

Take a few minutes to identify five negative beliefs that are not congruent with what you desire out of life. So stop reading and do this now.

My Limiting Beliefs

1. _____
2. _____
3. _____
4. _____
5. _____

Now that you've figured out some beliefs that have been limiting you from achieving your success, we're going to set them aside until we get to the next step.

Follow The Money

Lets talk about money. You bought this book called *The Ultimate Success Formula* and although it can be used to obtain a lot more than money, you probably want more money, too, right? So what beliefs do you have about money? Unless you are extremely wealthy and have more money than you can spend, you have some limiting beliefs about money or your worthiness to have more of it than you now have.

We covered a few of the many potentially limiting beliefs a person could have in this area in the previous example, but really think about it. What did you hear your parents say about money? What was the general feeling in your home while growing up pertaining to money? What did religious leaders, teachers and coaches say about money? What clichés did you hear repeatedly? What did your parents tell you when you asked for things? What did you experience in your past regarding money, wealth or lack?

Do you honestly believe that there's enough money for everyone? Do you believe that if you have more, somebody else has to have less? Do you believe that there's a limited amount of money that everyone has to divide? Are you afraid that there won't be enough left for you after everyone else takes their share? Do you believe that if you have a lot of money, your friends won't like you or will try to take advantage of you or will only want to hang around with you because of your money?

Do you believe that money corrupts people? Do you think money is good or is it evil? Do you believe you have to take advantage of other people to be rich? Do you think rich people are evil? Would you feel guilty about having a lot of money? Do you think it's wrong to be materialistic? Would you feel guilty about having a luxurious home, exotic automobiles, taking extravagant vacations, buying designer clothes or buying expensive jewelry and watches? Are you afraid you and/or your family wouldn't be safe if you were rich? What limiting beliefs do you have buried in your subconscious regarding money, wealth and riches?

All of these questions may feel overwhelming, but they will really help you uncover what's blocking you. By the way, a very insidious belief many people have is, "Money just isn't that important to me." Now stop and think about it for a second, if you said your spouse wasn't that important to you, how long would they stick around? Not long, right? Well, neither will money! You have to have healthy, productive and attractive beliefs about money if you're ever going to have it in abundance.

Take a few more minutes to brainstorm all of the beliefs, thoughts and ideas you have about money. Don't hold back. If there was ever a time to let all the negatives hang out, it is now. It will definitely serve you to find them so we can transform them to empower you!

My Limiting Money Beliefs

1. _____
2. _____
3. _____
4. _____
5. _____

Now that you have discovered many of the things that have been blocking you from having your success and dreams, let's not spend any more time living this reality. Follow me to the next step where you will learn how to remove these blocks once and for all.

Chapter 9

STEP FIVE: CLEAR AND ALIGN

The only thing limiting you in your life is your belief that you have limitations.

—Carlos Marin

It was believed in the past that the brain developed only in early childhood through a process called neurogenesis and the adult brain couldn't grow new brain cells or neural pathways. This was, in essence, the belief that you can't teach an old dog new tricks. However, the latest research has proven that neurogenesis occurs in the adult brain into our 70s and beyond. In fact, environmental enrichment and learning stimulate it while stress inhibits it.

The process known as neuroplasticity shows that we can create new neural pathways at any age. We can change the structure of our adult brain and our very behavior as well, at any age, by intentionally focusing our attention. That is what I'm going to show you how to do in this chapter by using some very powerful strategies that will help you focus intentionally on enriching, exciting, stimulating dreams while creating feelings of gratitude and happiness and reducing your stress and emotional baggage. You can transmute your limiting beliefs into empowering ones and science has proven this to be a fact. Let's dive in…

Question Your Beliefs

One way to transmute beliefs is to question the validity of the references that uphold that belief. If you remove the validity of the references, you change the belief or remove it altogether.

One of my old, limiting beliefs was: **I don't deserve success.**

Through the process I've shared with you, I remembered that my parents, grandparents and teachers were always telling me to, "slow down, you're still young, you still have a lot to learn and you have to pay the price for success."

When I acted impulsively or missed the mark, they would say, "Remember, you're still young and have a long way to go before you are ready to achieve real success." Consequently, I became really sensitive to the fact that I was too inexperienced and not good enough to attempt big things. They were actually saying this to console me and protect me when I messed up, but the message I heard in my subconscious mind was, 'I don't deserve success because I haven't learned everything I need to or paid the price yet.'

Later, when I started working in sales and would call on people, they'd say, "My gosh you're so young to be a financial planner." Even when it was a compliment, I was so self-conscious that it set off an unconscious trigger to my feelings of being undeserving and the belief

I had developed that, 'I'm not good enough yet so I don't deserve success.' As ridiculous as this may sound to you, this belief affected my level of confidence, self worth and my feeling of worthiness to attain high levels of success. It wasn't until I began questioning my beliefs that I realized I could change this.

Then I transmuted that belief to a really strong and empowering one:

I am as successful as I decide to be.

I began to realize that my success was a function of directing my mind towards my goals and maintaining a positive mental attitude, while executing my action blueprint in the faith that it is already done.

I changed my references by realizing that my limiting belief had been formed when I was young and wasn't even valid in the new context where it was affecting me, namely business success. I also realized that if I kept this belief, it would have very negative consequences in my life. It was keeping me broke!

The bottom line is that our beliefs can lead us to either create the life of our dreams or destroy our dreams and leave us with a life of misery. Therefore, we must purposely choose and transmute limiting beliefs into empowering ones!

This is a verse I read over 20 years ago and it's had a great impact in my life:

> If you think you are beaten, you are.
> If you think you dare not, you don't.
> If you'd like to win but think you can't,
> it is almost certain you won't.
> If you think you'll lose, you're lost.

For out in the world we find
Success begins with a fellow's will.
It's all in the state of mind.
If you think you're outclassed you are.
You've got to think high to rise.
You've got to be sure of yourself before
You can ever win the prize.
Life's battles don't always go
To the stronger or faster man,
But soon or late the man who wins
Is the man who thinks he can!
—**The Victor**, *C. W. Longenecker*

That, my friend, is the power of EMPOWERING BELIEFS.

My View on Empowering

Let's take a moment to discuss the word empowering, which I've used often throughout the book. I've specifically chosen this word and it's worthwhile to share the reason why. I do not believe there is a more powerful word in the English language than empower. It means drawing out of someone the strength, confidence, control, power and authority that resides within them. It is the ultimate freedom.

Here is a little back-story for you. I do trainings for both English and Spanish-speaking audiences. When I first started speaking, I would use the word empower, especially when talking about these new beliefs. In 1990, at an event in Mexico City, I was presenting on stage in front of a large Spanish-speaking crowd. Because I grew up in the United States and English became my first language, I usually think in English, and as I speak I need to translate on the spot. Early on in my career before I mastered the Spanish language, at speaking engagements I always had a translator there for support. At the point in my talk when I came to the word empower, I realized I did not know the Spanish translation. I asked my translator and his eyes kind of glazed over and I could tell he was thinking hard, searching for an answer. He then told me there is no literal translation. So I pressed him and asked, "What would you call it? What's the closest word?" He said, "Facilitate," and I thought, 'No way! That's not even close.' Facilitate sounded so wimpy. Facilitate or Empower? Huge difference. He then asked me, "Couldn't you just say give power?" No! Empower is not to give power. It's to bring forth the potential power that someone already has inside of them.

I was both frustrated and surprised that there wasn't a Spanish translation for empower. The more I studied language, I learned that it contains the strengths and weaknesses of the culture that communicates with it. The Anglo-Saxon language is very powerful and authoritative. The Spanish language is very poetic and romantic. Most translators take 20 to 30% more words to translate from English to Spanish.

That day, I decided I was still going to use empower and invented my own word in Spanish, empoderar, a literal translation from English. I explained to the audience what the word meant and why it was so important. I never compromised and used that word everywhere I spoke. A few years ago, a business associate told me that Royal Academy of Spain, the guardian of the official Spanish language, added empoderar to its dictionary. I went online and looked it up and sure enough it was there.

There is no other word that holds a candle to empower. Just recently, I was researching a charity that was of interest to me. I found a video clip on their website featuring former President Bill Clinton.

Regardless of your politics, this man has achieved monumental philanthropic goals that will benefit future generations. In his speech on this website, he was talking about empowerment, creating change and making a difference. Again, I realized the significance of the word empower to ignite passion and drive us forward on a global scale.

Eliminate Your Limiting References

You deserve to be empowered. Understand that the only things holding you back from achieving your greatness and all the riches you desire in life are your limiting beliefs and your resistance.

Think of a belief as a table. The top of the table is an idea or a thought. The legs are the references, distinctions and concepts that, through repetition, have given you a sense of certainty regarding the idea or thought.

Belief

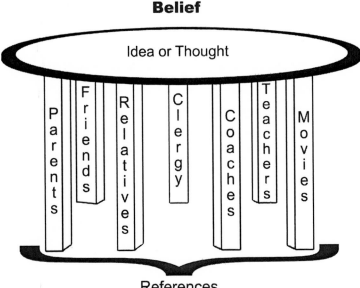

The idea or thought without the references would not be a belief, just an idea or thought. It's the references and the repetition of those references that create the sense of certainty that makes the idea a belief.

If you remove the references, you return the belief to an idea again and if you modify the idea and put new references or legs under it, you change the belief to an empowering one that serves you instead of one that limits you.

How do you remove the references? You start by asking the following questions of each belief that may be holding you back:

- Where did I learn this belief?
- Is this belief really true?
- Is this belief true in every context in my life?
- Is this belief serving me? Is it helping me be, do, have or give what I desire in life?
- Is this belief serving my loved ones and helping them have a better life?
- Is this belief serving mankind?
- What is ridiculous, absurd or funny about this belief?
- Does the person (or people) who taught me this belief have the results in their life that I desire in mine in this area?
- What will it cost me financially, physically, emotionally, in my relationships and with my loved ones if I don't change this belief?

I've taught people for years that one of the biggest mistakes you can make in life is to take advice from people who don't have what you want in that particular area. In my seminars, I kid around about how when most of us have a problem we usually go over to our buddy Joe, our next-door neighbor. Of course, he says, "Come on over here pal, tell old Joe your problems. Wait, let me get you a beer (so we can cry in our beer together)." And then you commiserate about how the boss is a jerk, life is unfair, your job sucks, the economy is going to hell in a hand basket, blah, blah, blah.

Now let me ask you a question, does your next-door neighbor have the kind of life that you want? How can he help you get ahead when he can't get ahead?

Let's take a look at another one of my old, limiting beliefs, one which many people (maybe even you) share also: You have to work really hard, struggle and sacrifice everything to succeed in life.

Limiting Belief

References

I've always loved to have fun and as a kid made a game out of everything. My parents used to say to me, "Who told you that you can have fun all the time? In life you have to work hard and sacrifice to succeed and if you have any time left over, then you can have fun." Eventually, I accepted this belief when I was a young man and resigned myself to the reality that my work life would be pure drudgery.

When I decided to purposely change my limiting beliefs and used this strategy on this belief, I realized that none of the people who taught me my references had anything near to the results I desired in my life, so why should I take their beliefs and limitations as true and make them mine? I shouldn't and I decided not to, so I removed all of those references. That left me with the idea: You have to work really hard and sacrifice to succeed in life, which now has no valid references supporting it.

Idea

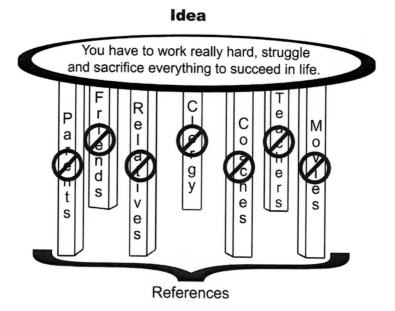

References

Eliminate the references that came from people who do not have the results or the life you want. It's that simple.

Create Empowering Beliefs

With my newfound clarity I looked for a new belief that would empower me to get what I desired in life. Ironically, I recalled that in everything I'd read about great successful people, they loved what they did, did it with passion and became rich. This was totally the opposite of how I'd been programmed. So I decided (key word here, my friend, it is by my choice now, not by conditioning) to create a new belief on purpose.

My new belief is:

To truly succeed in life you must do what you love with passion and excellence!

Does it resonate with me? Yeah, it makes me feel good to even say it and think about it.

It is critically important that you understand your beliefs must be congruent with your desires. Remember, we're creating a consciousness or state of mind that will automatically manifest what you desire and the secret to doing that is in having beliefs that produce those results.

It is not enough to identify what you want to change; you must decide what to replace it with and the easiest thing is to replace it with its positive opposite.

Find Supportive References

Now I look for references. And trust me, there are plenty. Check out a few of these millionaire and billionaires, each having fun living their purpose.

Bill Gates, cofounder of MicroSoft: Passionate about technology and software, uses his platform to give back on a global scale and loves what he does.

Richard Branson, founder of Virgin Group: Loves what he does and makes it an adventure, breaks new barriers, and is definitely passionate about it.

Marissa Mayer, Yahoo CEO and innovator: Constantly reinventing powerful brands, paving the way for women in business and loves what she does.

Donna Karan, award-winning fashion designer and founder of the Urban Zen Initiative: Uses her resources to fulfill her passion of advancing wellness, preserving culture and empowering children.

Ellen DeGeneres, television icon and entertainment pioneer: Inspires people around the world with her authenticity, humor and humanitarian efforts and exhibits passion in everything she does.

Donald Trump, real estate mogul: Even though I disagree with his dog-eat-dog philosophy, he is definitely passionate about what he does and loves doing it.

Oprah Winfrey, founder of the OWN Network: What can I say? Definitely loves what she does and does it with massive passion.

J.K. Rowling, creator and author of the mega-bestselling Harry Potter book series: Lives with purpose and gives back through various charitable organizations and philanthropic endeavors.

Mark Zuckerberg, founder of Facebook: Passionate about socializing and sharing information on the web and built a social media platform which now has over 1 billion users around the world.

Steve Jobs, cofounder of Apple and Pixar: In the 2005 Stanford Commencement speech stated, "The only way to be truly satisfied is to do great work and to do great work you must do what you love."

Is this not powerful proof that the new empowering belief that success is the result of doing what you love with passion and excellence is true?

Where do you get new, affirming references for other beliefs you want to create? From your own memory banks, from your own experience, from other people's experience — people you've seen succeed, get rich, have beautiful bodies, enjoy perfect health, have great relationships, experience love and joy. This is why reading inspiring stories, watching videos and listening to audios that describe other people's success is so powerful. You get to borrow them in order to create your own.

You can even pull them out of the future by imagining or visualizing yourself having those experiences or references. That's the purpose of your imagination; to create whatever end result you desire to achieve, just like magic. It's the most powerful tool you have and it doesn't cost you anything to use.

Let me ask you a question. How did Columbus discover America? Where did he get his references or sense of certainty that the world was round and not flat? He had to pull his references out of the future, something no one had seen before in the physical realm. He saw it in his mind, in his mental theater. He believed it so strongly that he was willing to risk his life and reputation.

When you do what you love, you vibrate at a very high frequency that attracts things that vibrate at high frequencies. Riches vibrate at high frequencies, as do all blessings and positive states. You infuse love into everything you do, and since love is the most powerful force in the universe, riches flow back to you multiplied many times over!

So now you set up these new references as the legs supporting your new belief: To truly succeed in life, do what you love with passion and excellence! And voilà, you have a new empowering belief!

Empowering Belief

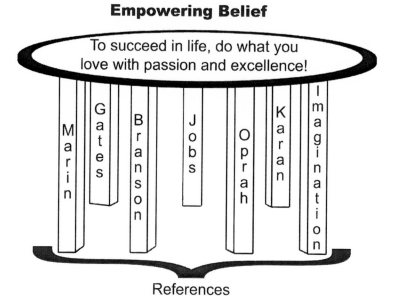

Transmuting YOUR Limiting Beliefs

In the last chapter you may have identified quite a few limiting beliefs and energy blocks that have been conditioned in you from an early age. Now we are ready to work on those blocks and transmute them into empowering beliefs and programs that will automatically take you where you want to go. In order to change a belief you must become aware of the limiting belief and also believe that:

- Something must change.
- I am the one who must change it.
- I have the power to change it.
- I must choose what to change it to.
- The new belief must be empowering and congruent with my Point B.

Take a moment to review your limiting beliefs and money beliefs that you identified in Step Four (Chapter 8). Choose the overall, top three, most destructive beliefs. We'll work on those now and once you get comfortable with the process, you can go back and work on the others.

If you need some help coming up with alternative, empowering beliefs, use these positive opposites of the old beliefs in the previous chapter as inspiration:

Limiting Belief: I'm too old / too young.

Empowering Belief: With age comes wisdom / youth is power.

Limiting Belief: I don't have enough education / the right education.

Empowering Belief: It's not how much you know, it's what you do with what you know that creates massive success.

Limiting Belief: I don't deserve success because of my past mistakes.

Empowering Belief: The past does not equal the future if I'm willing to learn from my mistakes.

Limiting Belief: People are against me / out to get me.

Empowering Belief: People reflect what I expect and they support me in my endeavors.

Limiting Belief: I'm black, Hispanic, white (I don't have the right ethnic background).

Empowering Belief: I deserve success for I am a child of God and He doesn't make junk.

Limiting Belief: I don't have time.

Empowering Belief: I make the time for what's important to me.

Limiting Belief: The economy is so bad that you can't make money today.

Empowering Belief: The biggest fortunes were created in so-called bad economies.

Limiting Belief: You have to have money to make money.

Empowering Belief: To make money you just need a big dream and persistent effort!

Limiting Belief: My duties as a mother / father (whatever) limit me or my spouse (partner) doesn't support me.

Empowering Belief: My success is the best example for my kids / spouse, etc.

Limiting Belief: I don't have the right skills.

Empowering Belief: Whatever I believe, I achieve and I can develop any skill I need to succeed.

Limiting Belief #1

_____

_____

_____

How has this belief limited your life?

_____

_____

_____

How is this belief not true?

_____

_____

_____

Who are the references? Do they have the results you want in this area?

_____

_____

_____

Who would you be without this belief?

_____

_____

_____

Empowering Belief #1

_____

_____

_____

How much better will your life be with this belief?

_____

_____

_____

How is this belief true?

_____

_____

_____

Who are the references that have the results you want?

_____

_____

_____

Who are you with this belief?

_____

_____

_____

Limiting Belief #2

_____

_____

_____

How has this belief limited your life?

_____

_____

_____

How is this belief not true?

_____

_____

_____

Who are the references? Do they have the results you want in this area?

_____

_____

_____

Who would you be without this belief?

_____

_____

_____

Empowering Belief #2

_____

_____

_____

How much better will your life be with this belief?

_____

_____

_____

How is this belief true?

_____

_____

_____

Who are the references that have the results you want?

_____

_____

_____

Who are you with this belief?

_____

_____

_____

Limiting Belief #3

_____

_____

_____

How has this belief limited your life?

_____

_____

_____

How is this belief not true?

_____

_____

_____

Who are the references? Do they have the results you want in this area?

_____

_____

_____

Who would you be without this belief?

_____

_____

_____

Empowering Belief #3

_____

_____

_____

How much better will your life be with this belief?

_____

_____

_____

How is this belief true?

_____

_____

_____

Who are the references that have the results you want?

_____

_____

_____

Who are you with this belief?

_____

_____

_____

Releasing Negative Emotions

How about when you just feel negative energy or emotion and cannot identify a belief that's blocking you? In addition to beliefs that we can actually pinpoint in our lives, many times things happened during childhood before we could even speak or understand. This is what happened in my story about leaving Cuba. I was not intellectually aware of what I believed; yet it was very real in my experience and it affected me for many years. This is energy stored in our bodies, in our subconscious mind, and we may not even be aware of it other than through a feeling of discomfort in certain situations.

When intense things happened, they might have caused extremely strong feelings or emotions that we now label trauma. These intense emotions create indescribable sensations that move us in ways that seem unreasonable to the logical, conscious mind. Nevertheless, they are very real in our inner world and their effects can be certainly felt in our outer world.

It is important that when we feel negative feelings or emotions, we acknowledge and release them in order to center ourselves and direct our energy positively. Whenever we feel bad it is because what we're thinking is not in alignment with our higher self. This divinely endowed part of us knows we are unlimited potential and worthy of all good, success, wealth, wholeness and happiness. So a negative feeling is really an alarm that there is some fear, negative belief or program running in your subconscious and to prompt you to get back on the right track and be congruent with your true self, your chosen identity, your dreams and intentions.

The key to purposely directing your emotional states is to get into the habit of consciously catching yourself any time you feel bad. Then simply release the negative emotion you're experiencing with one of several powerful strategies I'll teach you and refocus your thoughts.

The Power of Release

Before we begin the all-important work of releasing your emotional blocks, I want to share another story with you.

> Betty was a skeptical attendee at one of my seminars. She was an attractive woman, but it was her eyes that drew my attention because they conveyed a deep sadness. During the first day she came up to me and said she was having trouble with the exercises because she didn't know what she wanted. I talked with her for a while and told her to pretend that she did know and do the exercises acting as if she did. On the second day, we began teaching release techniques to remove emotional blocks. (The techniques I teach at my live seminars are quite intense and can be emotionally charged, so they're best suited for a setting where I can personally guide you through issues to produce immediate positive results. I highly encourage you to attend one of my events or online programs and experience this level of empowerment for yourself.)
>
> After several hours of watching other people release on major issues and feeling herself opening up at a new level, Betty came up to the front of the room and asked if I could work with her next. She wanted to break through and felt safe in the environment of the group. As soon as we started applying an energy psychology technique called Meridian Tapping (which is like acupuncture without needles), she started crying and talking a mile a minute about her emotional scars. It turned out she had been consistently sexually abused from the ages of eight to 14

and had suffered assault as a young woman as well. As you can imagine, she was buried under years of pain and fear.

That day, as she released the feelings of unworthiness, self-blame and guilt, Betty's countenance began to change in front of our eyes. She looked 10 years younger and the audience was amazed! She replaced anxiety with peace, love and harmony. She relinquished fear for abundance, confidence and power. She forgave and accepted herself and experienced an incredible transformation. Betty then began getting clear on what she wanted for her life. Today she has a highly successful business that brings her tremendous satisfaction and happiness and she is helping other abused women overcome their traumas.

That is the power of releasing emotional blocks!

5 Powerful Release Strategies

Release Strategy One: Simple Clearing Method

One of the fastest strategies to release negative emotion is to welcome the feeling or belief that popped up and say to yourself, 'I welcome (or love) you, my feeling, emotion, belief, and I am grateful for the opportunity to free you and myself.'

When you begin the process it's a good idea to rate the intensity of the emotion on a scale of 1 to 10 with 1 being no emotion and 10 being off the charts, that way you can gauge it as you release. It's also helpful to scan your body and notice where you are feeling the emotion (usually stomach area or solar plexus) and focus your attention there, even putting your hand there, while you welcome the emotion and express gratitude for the opportunity to release it and free yourself.

As you do this, oftentimes an involuntary sigh or releasing breath will occur. That's a sign that you are letting go of the pent up energy. Then check yourself again on the intensity of the remaining emotion on a scale of 1 to 10. Simply repeat until you're at a three or below.

Why should you welcome an emotion or feeling that you don't want? First of all, because if it popped up, you have it inside and it's making you feel bad or limiting you. It's already in you. Do you want to keep it or get rid of it? Get rid of it, right? Suppressing a feeling or emotion is keeping it; it's bottling it up and driving it deep down inside you. The key with all of these clearing techniques is that you release the belief, feeling or emotion.

Remember that everything in this universe is energy. Thoughts, feelings and emotions are energy. For goodness sake, emotion means energy in motion and when you bottle it up and don't let it flow like it wants to and is supposed to, you create dis-ease. That's where sickness and disease come from. So, learn some of these techniques that you can use on the fly. I know it may sound a little strange if you've never heard about releasing techniques before (it certainly did to me at first), but believe me it works like a charm!

Let's say you're in a business meeting with several people to win over an important prospective client and one of your associates, with whom you have a bit of a competitive relationship, makes a negative comment regarding competency, directed subtly at you. All of a sudden you are really pissed off and at the same time your fear of rejection rears its ugly head. You are feeling anger, hatred, fear and resentment and maybe even revenge and if you get up and excuse yourself you're afraid you'll look weak, so what do you do?

While sitting right there you take a deep breath and put a little smile on your face, go inside and say to yourself with feeling, 'I love you my dear emotions and I am grateful for this opportunity to free all of you and myself.' You'll find yourself feeling better immediately, although you may need to focus your attention on the emotion while saying the release phrase to yourself two or three times before you're back to being fully balanced.

If you want to become an expert at releasing negative emotions I highly recommend a course called The Sedona Method. Hale Dwoskin, CEO of Sedona Training Associates, learned the strategy from its creator, Lester Levinson, a physicist who at age 42 was dying from numerous health complications. Levinson, understanding how energy flowed, decided to embark on a journey to release all the negative energy he had within him. In a matter of three months of non-stop releasing, he had cured himself. He then set out to share his discovery with the world. Hale was one of his best students who, after Lester's passing over 40 years later, is carrying on his great work teaching people to liberate themselves from the emotional traumas and blocks that are keeping them from having a joyous life.

Release Strategy Two: Power Affirmations

While you may have heard of this next strategy before I encourage you to consider it with fresh eyes and ears as it is a source of power for some of the most successful people in the world. It is critical that you develop a series of powerful affirmations to remind you of who you really are, so you can direct your thinking and mental conversations to transform yourself. You can go from zero to superhero almost overnight.

You may be thinking that affirmations don't work for you. That may be because you're actually repeating negative words and thoughts, which are negative affirmations, far more consistently than any positive ones. According to the Laboratory of Neuro Imaging at UCLA, the average person has over 70,000 thoughts per day and over 90% of them are the same thoughts day in and day out. What many people don't understand is that a repeated thought becomes a <u>declaration of truth</u> to the subconscious mind. If it's negative, it is a negative affirmation that must produce its material equivalent. For many people, this is an unconscious process, and they simply are not aware of what they're thinking, when they're thinking it, or how often they're thinking it.

Let me share with you a series of affirmations that I began using when I was still broke and in debt, but working on my burning desire to be a millionaire.

- I am an extension of Infinite Intelligence.
- God is my unlimited source and supply; therefore I am wealthy and always have a divine surplus.
- I can do all things through God within me, which is my power and everything I do succeeds.
- I am a multi-millionaire. I am financially free and debt free.
- I have a reliable, fast growing income of over $1 million dollars a year.
- I have the fastest growing marketing network in the world.
- I am helping thousands of people become financially free with my success principles and businesses.

I would affirm this declaration as soon as I got up in the morning and over 50 times a day, like a mantra, until it filled my consciousness and became a fixed part of my mindset. It wasn't long thereafter that I started acting as if it was true and producing massive positive results in my life.

In the early 1900s, Charles Haanel, author of the book, *Master Key System*, used principle-based affirmations to help his students align their minds and create positive results. Some say he was advanced in his thinking because he taught that thoughts and words are creative energy, which automatically correlate with their object and manifest it because thought is spiritual energy. He said that prosperity was the result of right or creative thinking and poverty was the result of negative or destructive thinking. Every negative thought or word is destructive and must not be allowed to enter your mind or be expressed in words.

Haanel gave people the following affirmation and told them to say it first thing every morning and last thing before going to bed at night and as many times as possible throughout the day, "I am whole, perfect, strong, powerful, loving, harmonious, prosperous and happy." I have personally used this affirmation and it is extremely powerful!

Dr. Émile Coué, French psychologist and pharmacist, became famous for innumerable remarkable cures in his clinic by suggesting that the power of healing lies within the patient himself. The secret of success in this treatment was to create confidence in the conscious mind that what it repeats with feeling is accepted by the subconscious mind and is transformed by it into reality, forming a permanent element (belief) that will continue to automatically produce congruent results. The primary affirmation that he taught all of his patients was, "Every day in every way I'm getting better and better!" This powerful all-encompassing affirmation later became one of the foundations of Dr. Jose Silva's world famous, Silva Mind Control Method, which has changed the lives of millions of people.

Everyone who has achieved great success uses some form of affirmation in his or her life. The best example of this is even in music today. Listen to the lyrics by some of your favorite artists and tell me what you hear! From power couple, Beyoncé and Jay Z, to The

Beatles, to Lady Gaga! And if they use affirming statements in their songs, I have a pretty strong feeling they use them in other areas of their life, too!

Suze Orman, personal financial guru, television host and bestselling author, publicly acknowledges the power of affirmations in her life. She has talked openly about her early start when she worked in a bakery and made only $400 a month. Initially wanting to run her own restaurant, it was a series of financial setbacks on the road to this dream that lead her to Wall Street. As one of the only women in her firm and with the odds stacked against her, Orman learned to control her thoughts, change her thinking and master the market. Her most famous affirmation is, "I have more money than I will ever need." She has told her viewers to repeat that mantra, or a similar one of their own, over and over again until they believe it to be true.

Boxing legend and three-time heavyweight champion of the world, Muhammad Ali, once stated "It's the repetition of affirmations that leads to belief. And once that belief becomes a deep conviction, things begin to happen." He also said, "I am the greatest. I said that even before I knew I was." He used positive affirmations to build his belief in himself and intimidate his opponents!

Lebron James and the Miami Heat basketball team, who have won back-to-back NBA Championships, use a team battle cry, which is an affirmation, before and during each game to focus and inspire them. This powerful declaration, "To the last minute, to the last second, to the last man we fight," is indicative of a team that had a 27-game winning steak throughout 2013, coming from behind to win again and again. In the finals, after being down three games to two against the San Antonio Spurs, they came back from a huge deficit to win game six in overtime and game seven in the last 40 seconds, to clinch the NBA championship.

I use affirmations to remind me of who I am and the unlimited potential that I have within me. They build my faith and give me strength to continually move forward towards my dreams because they are universal truth.

Let's say that you are having financial difficulties and are stressed about paying your mortgage or your bills. Your main focus is to impress your mind with the idea of abundance, which is really part of your birthright. These affirmations will allow you to accomplish that:

- God is my unlimited source and supply. Therefore, I have an abundant supply of money and always have a divine surplus.
- By day and by night I am being prospered in all of my interests. Every day in every way I'm getting richer and richer.
- My sales are improving every day. I am progressing, advancing and getting wealthier every day.

Suppose you dislike your job, have issues with your boss or your business is on the rocks and you want to change your situation. You might use one of these affirmations:

- The divine plan for my life is a perfect idea in Infinite Intelligence, which is irrefutable, incorruptible and invincible and is now rapidly coming to pass in my life.
- I am now rapidly expanding into the divine plan for my life and am enjoying perfect self-expression.

- I expect the miraculous and it happens now. My seemingly impossible good has come to pass.

If the problem is a health issue, you might use one of the following:

- My body is a perfect idea in Infinite Intelligence and therefore is whole and perfect.
- Every day in every way I'm getting healthier and healthier.
- I cast this burden of (whatever your issue is) on my God-self within me and I go free to enjoy perfect wholeness and divine health.

In all cases, the key is to repeat these affirmations of truth with deep feeling over and over. Remember, what you are doing is impressing the subconscious mind with these suggestions through repetition and deep feeling. You can combine any of these with your I Am Declarations to create your own Power Affirmations. Make sure the affirmations resonate with you, if not, reword them until they do and make them your own. Another very important aspect is to say these phrases right before going to sleep at night so that your subconscious (which never sleeps) is working to produce them in your life while your conscious mind is sleeping.

Release Strategy Three:
Interrupt Your Negative Patterns

A very valuable skill to acquire is that of interrupting the negative thought pattern. One way is to catch yourself any time your self-talk goes negative or you start worrying. Do you remember when people would wear a rubber band around their wrist? Then if they said a bad word or did something they didn't want to do, they snapped the band? Do you know of anyone who actually changed behavior using this technique? While I know numerous people who have, I'm not suggesting you inflict bodily harm on yourself every time you think negatively. Instead, let's create a positive pattern interrupt to get your focus back on what you desire.

As soon as you notice you are worrying, say something like, "Hey, I'm worrying! I'm focusing on what I don't want." Which means, "I'm using the Law of Attraction in reverse!" Then change your focus to what you desire. That's why it's important to clearly define who you are committed to being and what you're committed to having. In doing so, you've got some clearly defined objectives to switch your focus to in an instant.

Create a few pattern interrupts that resonate with you in advance, so when you catch yourself thinking the wrong thing, you can break your pattern. This can be goofy and fun, depending on who you are, your style and sense of humor.

You can come up with any type of phrase that feels good to you. Maybe you aspire to be like superstar Angelina Jolie. When you catch yourself doing something out of character, say, "This is so *not* Angelina." Or if mega musician and actor Justin Timberlake is more your speed, you may say something like, "Why am I thinking this way? I need to bring sexy back." Perhaps you prefer comic strip super heroes, so you may say, "I'm Iron Man. I'm not afraid of anything!" You get where I'm going with this?

My Pattern Interrupts

_____

_____

_____

_____

_____

_____

_____

_____

_____

Release Strategy Four: Gratitude and Happiness

Most people believe that when they are more successful then they'll be happy. When they have more money then they'll be happy. Or when their spouse treats them better or when they lose 25 pounds then they'll be happy. Recent discoveries in the field of positive psychology and neuroscience are showing that the exact opposite is true. Happiness and positive thinking are what fuel success!

Shawn Achor spent over a decade at Harvard University, researching and teaching happiness to thousands of students. He then started a consulting firm to teach the principles he'd learned to Fortune 500 executives in over 50 countries. His books *The Happiness Advantage* and *Before Happiness* document and explain the fantastic results of his works in both worlds. They provide actionable techniques that you can immediately apply to use happiness and gratitude to create greater levels of success in your life!

In addition to the statements and declarations you listed above, I find it helpful to also have at least 10 things you're grateful for and make you feel really good. It can be your relationship with God, your soul mate, your children, your cat or dog, the sound of the ocean, a place you love to visit or something you love to do. It's all about feeling good, grateful or happy and these things will raise your vibration quickly. When you vibrate at a high frequency, you attract other good things that are also vibrating at a high frequency.

Good Vibe Questions

Along with gratitude and happy thoughts, I've also developed a series of Good Vibe Questions to ask myself that immediately change my focus, raise my vibration and improve the way I feel. I originally learned these questions from Tony Robbins and have made my own modifications that I resonate more with over the years. These questions also are a great way to start or end your day feeling good and full of positive energy. Remember, what you attract into your life is based on your vibration.

1. What am I happy about? Why does that make me happy?
2. What am I grateful for? Why does that make me feel grateful?
3. What am I enjoying in my life? Why do I enjoy that so much?
4. What am I most excited about? Why does that excite me?
5. What am I most committed to? Why am I committed to that?
6. What am I proud of? Why does that make me feel proud?
7. Who do I love? What about them makes me feel love?

These questions are a great way to raise your vibration anytime you're feeling down or negative. They work instantly!

Remember, if you feel bad, you're thinking negatively or you're focused on what you lack. When you feel good, you're thinking positively and are focused on what you're grateful for and you desire. So manage your emotional states and maintain a high vibrational frequency to attract all good into your life. The key to this strategy is whenever you catch yourself feeling bad, immediately switch your thoughts to one of the things that make you feel happy or grateful or ask one of the Good Vibe Questions and you'll immediately raise your vibration! So right now, write down 10 things you are grateful for or make you feel happy just thinking about them:

My 10 Gratitude and Happy Thoughts

_____
_____
_____
_____
_____
_____
_____
_____
_____
_____

How are you feeling? I don't know about you, but my heart is full after I focus on gratitude. Even when you are going through a difficult time, you can always find something to appreciate. If you're stuck, start with your breath. Close your eyes, and as you focus on each intake and exhale of air, be grateful for this amazing function of your body. Every breath of gratitude will enable you to release any negative energy and lead you to recognize the other miracles in your life. So pay attention, and from this place of centeredness, you will open yourself up to extraordinary healing.

Release Strategy Five: Meridian Tapping

One of the most powerful strategies I have found to change limiting beliefs, release emotional trauma and eliminate psychological reversal is a cutting edge technique called Meridian Tapping. This is actually a form of energy psychology based on healing concepts that have been practiced in Eastern medicine for over 5,000 years. Most energy psychologists agree that the cause of all negative emotions is a disruption in the body's energy system. The body, just like everything else in the universe, is made up of energy and if you restore the balance to the body's energy system, you will eliminate the negative emotions and their underlying beliefs, which caused the energy disruption.

At the root of Chinese acupuncture are the 400+ energy points and 20 meridians connecting them, which can be stimulated in order to heal the body. Acupuncture does that by placing needles in these points thereby releasing the blocked energy causing the disruption in the body's energy field. Acupressure releases the energy by applying pressure alone on the meridian points. This is the principle that meridian tapping is based on and I have found it to be highly effective.

The basic strategy is to focus on the negative emotion, fear, memory or belief that is making you feel bad and blocking what you desire. While maintaining your mental focus on the problem or belief, use your fingertips to tap five to seven times on each of eight of the body's meridian points to release the negative charge.

Here's how it works.

Step One: Identify

Identify the problem or belief you want to transmute and think about it. How do you feel about it right now? Rate the intensity level of your feeling about this problem, emotion or belief with 1 being the lowest level and 10 the most intense.

Step Two: Set Up

Most of the time these beliefs, emotions or feelings that are blocking you are in conflict with what you want in your life, which as you know means you are psychologically reversed. To deal with and eliminate the reversal you start tapping on the karate chop point of your hand, which is the fleshy part of the outside of your palm where you would chop a board in karate. You tap there with three or four fingers repeatedly while stating the issue, belief or problem and then follow it up with an unconditional love and acceptance affirmation of yourself in order to release the energy.

So you would say something like: "Even though I have this (problem, issue, feeling, emotion, belief, phobia, etc.) I deeply and completely forgive, accept and love myself anyway."

You do this three times to deal with the conflicting beliefs between your conscious and subconscious mind.

Some people will question, "I thought you weren't supposed to make any negative affirmations or statements? I don't want to attract any more negative conditions than I already have."

I will assure you that is not the case, as your subconscious already has a belief that is limiting and holding you back from having what you consciously desire. This strategy is acknowledging it, while also loving and accepting yourself even though you have this conflict. It is amazing how quickly this technique will resolve a conflict in beliefs.

Step Three: Tapping Points

I must make it clear to you that this is very powerful stuff and it could bring out emotions that might be uncomfortable at this moment, so you must take full responsibility for your own well-being and tap at your own risk.

Look at the tapping points on the illustration to see where to tap. As you tap on these points you'll repeat a short reminder phrase to access the correct file from your mind that is related to the set up phrase you used in the previous step, such as *my money issue* or *my fear of rejection* or *my fear of failure*. Do this tapping for a couple of rounds or sequences to get comfortable with the process. Once you begin to feel like you're in a flow, you can move into some more advanced positive reinforcement tapping illustrated here.

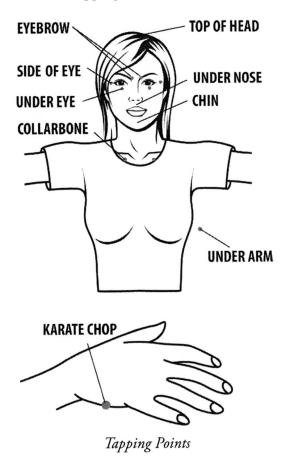

Tapping Points

Eyebrow Point (EB) is the bony area at the front corner of your eyebrow as it dips down towards your nose.

Side of Eye (SE) is the dip of your eye socket approximately one inch from the corner of your eye.

Under Eye (UE) the hard area under the eye that merges with the cheekbone, approximately ½ inch under your eye.

Under Nose (UN) is the area half way between your nose and your upper lip.

Chin (CH) is the area half way between your bottom lip and chin near where the cleft is.

Collarbone (CB) is the area on either side of your collarbone or you can tap with your fist in the middle right where the U at the base of your neck is.

Under Arm (UA) is the area where a woman's bra would be approximately about six inches under the armpit. In men it is where the lat muscle is.

Crown of Head (H) is the center and top of the head. It is where you would wear a crown if you were king or where my Jewish friends would wear their Yarmulkes.

When you tap on the tapping points, you should use a firm yet gentle pressure as if you were testing a melon to see if it's ripe. You can use all four fingers or just two, index and middle fingers. Four fingers are generally used for the top of the head, collarbone, under the arm or wider areas. On sensitive areas like around the eyes, you can use just two. Tap with your fingertips and not with your fingernails. The tapping order begins at the top and works down.

If you're thinking this tapping stuff is kind of weird, I know how you feel because that's exactly how I felt when my wife Cecy first showed it to me over six years ago. She had been researching techniques to release emotional trauma on the Internet and came across some information on it. She watched some videos showing how to apply the technique and started using it on herself. It seemed so goofy when I saw her doing it that I had a hard time believing it could work. After all I couldn't see myself in my seminars tapping on my head, face and chest!

It was when I saw the results she was getting using it to get rid of migraine headaches that I did some research on it. When I saw the very credible people that were endorsing it such as Jack Canfield, Bob Proctor, Dr. Bruce H. Lipton, Bob Doyle and Dr. Joe Vitale, to name a few, I had to try it. I began to use and test it on myself and the people I work with. The results were so absolutely amazing that I incorporated it into my transformational seminars.

Since I'm not there live with you to know your specific issue I'll walk you through an example of which most people can relate. And if you want to follow this process visually instead of reading it, create an account at http://CarlosMarin.com/usf and click on Videos for the complete *Tapping Session* exercise that you can follow along as I guide you. [Once you have created an account, a temporary password will be emailed to you. Thereafter, you can access all bonus content through the login page at http://usfbook.carlosmarin.com/login. Simply enter your email and password.]

Are you ready? Then let's get this party started...

Step One: Identify
For this example, let's focus on your feelings towards money. Do you believe it's hard to get rich? Rate your level of intensity around the issue of making money from 1 to 10.

Step Two: Set Up

Tap the karate chop part of your hand and say, "Even though I believe it's hard to get rich, I choose to forgive, accept and love myself."

Keep tapping the karate chop part of your hand and now say: "Even though I believe it's hard to get rich and it is keeping me from being all I can be, having all I can have and doing all I can do, I deeply and completely forgive, accept and love myself anyway."

Keep tapping the karate chop part of your hand and say: "Even though I believe it's hard to get rich and it's causing me to suffer in life and feel deprived and it's keeping me from giving my loved ones everything they deserve which makes me feel broke and like I'm not good enough, I deeply and completely forgive myself, accept and honor myself and love myself unconditionally."

Step Three: Tapping

Now let's move through the other tapping points.

Eyebrow Point: It's hard to get rich
Side of Eye: It's really hard to get rich
Under Eye: No matter what I do
Under Nose: I can't get myself to get rich
Under Mouth: It's so hard to get rich
Collarbone: So very hard to be rich
Under Arm: And I feel broke
Crown of Head: And not good enough to be rich
Eyebrow Point: It's hard to get rich
Side of Eye: It's really hard to get rich
Under Eye: No matter what I do
Under Nose: I can't get myself to get rich

Under Mouth: It's so hard to get rich

Collarbone: And even though I feel deprived

Under Arm: And I feel broke

Crown of Head: And not good enough to be rich

Eyebrow Point: I choose to allow myself to feel rich

Side of Eye: I allow myself to feel rich

Under Eye: I am letting go of the belief that it's hard to be rich

Under Nose: I am letting it go right now

Under Mouth: Because it's keeping me broke

Collarbone: I am letting go of the belief

Under Arm: That it's really hard to get rich

Crown of Head: Because I know of many people that are rich

Eyebrow Point: And I deserve to be rich too

Side of Eye: Therefore I choose to feel rich

Under Eye: Because there's abundance all around me

Under Nose: And I choose to see it and know that it's there for me

Under Mouth: For my pleasure and enjoyment

Collarbone: What God has done for others He now does for me and more

Under Arm: The walls of lack and delay have crumbled away

Crown of Head: And I receive my riches now

Now notice how you're feeling. On a scale of 1 to 10 where are you? You should have seen a significant decrease in the intensity of your emotion regarding that belief. Depending on how strong the belief was you may need to go through the sequence several times. This time in the set-up you'd say, "Even though I have this *remaining* feeling that it's hard to get rich, I deeply and completely forgive myself, etc."

By the way, you should drink plenty of water whenever you tap as you're moving energy in your body and for maximum benefit you need to be well hydrated.

While it's best to tap saying the phrases out loud, you can also say them to yourself in your mind, which is still very effective, especially if you have an intense emotion or feeling happening in the moment. For in-depth training on meridian tapping as well as all the belief transmuting and releasing strategies I teach, check out my comprehensive program *The Unlimited Success Academy* at http://UnlimitedSuccessAcademy.com.

Putting it All Together— The Alignment Strategy

If you're feeling empowered right now, that's fantastic! At the very least, I hope you're feeling optimistic. I know you can do this. You can take control of your emotional states and live your life on purpose, every day.

Remember we talked about the power of compounding? It especially applies to the release strategies we've just discussed. When you combine one or more of the strategies together, in real-time, and add in a few of the best practices you've completed so far, you will create long-term patterns of recognition, release and empowerment. I call this the **Alignment Strategy**. It is your moment-to-moment process to support you every single day.

The Bible talks about "being transformed by the renewing of your mind" (Rom. 12:2), which is the result of what and how you think consistently. To be renewed you must think new and different thoughts that are in alignment with the person you want to be and the results you want to produce. This strategy is the tool to help you do just that. Here's how it works.

1. **Be Conscious of Your Feelings**

   Stop and check in with yourself often and become aware of your emotional states. Be present and notice when you are feeling bad, anxious, jealous, scared, fearful, worried or depressed.

2. **Release the Negative Emotions**

   Use one of the five techniques you've just learned to release and raise your vibration.
   - Strategy One: Simple Clearing Method
   - Strategy Two: Power Affirmations
   - Strategy Three: Interrupt Your Negative Patterns
   - Strategy Four: Gratitude and Happiness
   - Strategy Five: Meridian Tapping

   Take it a step further by combining one or more of them for maximum impact. (e.g., Clearing Method followed by Power Affirmations or Pattern Interrupt followed by Tapping and Gratitude)

3. **Refocus Your Thoughts and Align with Your True Self**

   Here is where it gets fun! Compound your results by using any or all of the techniques from earlier in the book. Repeat your:
   - Identity Statement
   - Purpose Statement
   - I Am Declarations
   - Tapping while declaring any of these is very powerful!

4. **Act with Total Power and Confidence**

   Know that you already are the person who is, does, has and gives what you desire and then make it happen. (You will learn how to create a *Power Trigger* to get you there instantaneously in Step Seven.)

If this seems a bit overwhelming, please understand that once you master these steps you can do this Alignment Strategy in minutes or even seconds. The latest research on the brain shows that the more you do processes that reduce stress and stimulate creativity you create new neural pathways that make it easier and even automatic in the future. Through repetition, the words and images that resonate the most with you will already be in your mind and on your lips. Does your Purpose Statement get you fired up? Great, use that. Maybe when you think your Purpose, you naturally roll into your top I Am Declarations. Perfect! Find the order and sequence that supports your needs and works best for you, but at the beginning, I encourage you to use them all.

Remember when you first learned to drive a car? All of the steps you now do unconsciously before you pull out of the driveway— adjusting your seat, checking the side/rearview mirrors, fastening your seatbelt, looking both ways, turning the key in the ignition, slowly releasing the break and putting your foot on the gas pedal— were very overwhelming. But the more you drove and as your confidence rose, soon they became second nature. Now you don't need 10 minutes before you put the car in motion. You go through the mental checklist in your mind, sometimes while carrying on a conversation with a passenger or taking a sip of coffee. It'll be the same with the Alignment Strategy once it becomes a habit. And how's this for bonus? The more you are tuned into your emotional states, the more you will learn the potential triggers that set off your negative emotions and be able to use the Alignment Strategy proactively before a situation escalates.

Had I known this powerful strategy earlier I would have saved myself a lot of time, produced exponentially greater results and empowered millions of more people. However, the good news is both you and I know it now so we can use it to produce phenomenal results from today forward!

Chapter 10

STEP SIX: CREATE AN ACTION BLUEPRINT

You were born to win, but to be a winner, you must plan to win, prepare to win, and expect to win.

—Zig Ziglar

How Big Is Your Dream?

Early in my career, one of my original mentors, Bill Childers, used to always say, "If the dream is big enough, the facts don't count." Bill was a big dreamer with great vision and he taught me that without a big vision a man will not achieve anything and will die broke and in mediocrity.

No dream is ever too big!

Do you have a goal that really moves you, that floats your boat and turns you on? In order for you to have the level of success you desire and the motivation to go for it you must have a huge vision attached to a major goal. For many people, it's associated with their career, particularly if their career is aligned with their purpose. For people whose career is not aligned with their purpose, this goal is usually to create a new career that allows them to live their purpose, enjoy life and contribute to mankind.

This is the goal that makes your dreams a reality and gets you your Point B lifestyle. It motivates you to get up in the morning, excited about life. It's what you're passionate about and it drives you to give your all, regardless of time, effort or criticism. I call this your Ultimate Goal.

It's tremendously important to define this Ultimate Goal because this will help you maintain your focus and drive your actions towards where you want to go. It's also important to understand that this Ultimate Goal, which is in line with your purpose and is what you want most in life right now, once attained, will be replaced with what you want most at that time. In other words, you will create a new Ultimate Goal.

This process is dynamic. Let me explain with my own story.

When I first started in network marketing, it took me three-and-a-half years to understand this principle. Once I did and defined my Ultimate Goal, it took me two-and-a-half years to attain that goal, and that goal made me a millionaire.

Not knowing what I know now, I didn't immediately replace the first goal with another major goal for over two years, during which time I was frustrated. Achieving this first major goal got me over my own personal needs, which made me comfortable. Not replacing it with another Ultimate Goal made me unfocused and confused about what I wanted in life.

Then I discovered my purpose and got a new Ultimate Goal. I felt focused and recharged once again as I worked passionately towards my dreams. My organization grew from 10,000 to 500,000 distributors and my income grew over 2,000% in less than five years.

Today I have a new Ultimate Goal that is congruent with who I am and my purpose in life that I'm totally passionate about and that drives me. This book is a part of that purpose and Ultimate Goal.

How's that for a motive so compelling that it drives you to take action? Now it's your turn to find your own Ultimate Goal.

Right now, take a couple of minutes to go back and review all of the goals and intentions you've written from the exercises in this book, including your Identity Statement (Chapter 5) and your Purpose Statement (Chapter 6). It will also be helpful to review your I Am Declarations from Step Three (Chapter 7). My experience has proven that most people's Ultimate Goal is a longer term dream that most of us feel will take around five years to achieve. So search deep for that goal or achievement that you feel will make all of your dreams a reality.

Great! So how do you feel after seeing who you are so far? Do you already know what your Ultimate Goal is? Have you at least started to get a feeling about it?

I hope there is a feeling growing inside of you right now. It's the birth of a dream, something that's really going to drive your life. It's a motive so strong that it will compel you to take massive action and have fun doing it.

Maybe it's a...

- Business of your own, achieving a level of business volume, sales or recognition.
- Position you want to attain in your company, a promotion in position/rank or taking your company public.
- Charitable organization you want to build or one you want to fund.
- Major change you want to bring into this world, a positive transformation in saving the environment or in the consciousness of mankind.
- Level of income or investments, certain net worth, specific amount of assets, or being debt/financially free.
- Educating great, independent kids.

To give you an idea, here is my first Ultimate Goal from 1986:

I am totally committed to achieving my Ultimate Goal of being a millionaire by August 1, 1988.

Whatever it is, write it down now, along with <u>a date for its attainment</u>. Take as much time as you need. Determine what your most compelling goal is and make it definite.

My Ultimate Goal
I am totally committed to achieving my Ultimate Goal of

_____

_____

_____

_____

By: _____

Now, I want you to write down why you want to achieve this goal. Make the reasons compelling. Remember, when you know your <u>Why</u>, you'll always figure out the <u>How</u>.

- What will achieving this goal do for you?
- What will it do for your family?
- What will it contribute to mankind?
- How will it make this world a better place to live?
- How will it make you feel?
- How will it make your loved ones feel?

Here are my why reasons for achieving my Ultimate Goal back in 1986:

Achieving this goal will give my family and I financial freedom. I will buy us a 5,000 square foot home on two acres of land with a resort style pool, a BMW 745 il for me and a Lincoln Navigator for my wife. I will buy us his and hers gold Rolex watches and new high fashion wardrobes. I will provide my little girls the best lifestyle they can ever imagine, homeschool them and they will have a full time daddy. I will give over $100,000 per year to my church and charities I believe in. I will provide my family the best lifestyle they deserve.

Write down all of your compelling reasons for achieving this goal. Do this now. Don't put it off until later because this is important stuff. It's creating your future on purpose that we're talking about here!

My Compelling WHY

_____

_____

_____

_____

_____

_____

_____

_____

_____

_____

_____

_____

_____

Write Your Own Script

Now that you've decided what the ending of your story is going to be, we need to start writing the script as to how it happens. I want you to know that I'm a big believer in allowing the universe to provide the answers and make the path. However, I also believe we need to start moving and acting like we already are, do, have and give what we desire in order for Providence to move! It's all about your Action Blueprint.

One of the most productive people on the planet is my friend and mentor Alex Mandossian. Alex is a master trainer, speaker, productivity expert and the world's foremost guru on doing lucrative teleseminars.

His program, Teleseminar Secrets, is where I, and many of the top marketers in the world, learned to do them effectively.

Alex always teaches that where attention goes, energy flows so you've got to stay focused on the actions that produce measurable results in your business and life. He creates very specific frameworks in all of his programs that produce real-world results and teaches his students to create highly effective action plans to increase their productivity and achieve their goals more quickly. He has personally used his action strategies to turn his annual income into his weekly income in a handful of years. Needless to say, I highly recommend his programs.

Let me share another story of one of my mentees, Albert, which further illustrates the power of creating an effective Action Blueprint:

Albert was a middle-aged executive for a large multi-national corporation in Europe. He had spent years climbing the corporate ladder and, having reached what had been painted to him as the top, was frustrated and restless. He longed to be in control of his own future instead of being dictated to by overseas executives and faceless shareholders. When we first met he had already been involved in my business for a while and had achieved moderate success. However, coming from the corporate world many things, especially the lack of structure, did not make sense to him. He felt the limited success he had in our business was not what it should be for the time he was investing.

I agreed with him and explained that he was spending too much time in the wrong activities and not working in the right places. When I sat down and laid out a definite plan of action for him based on his current organization's structure his jaw hit the floor. For the first time he realized that that there was a precise science to building marketing organizations, you just had to learn it from someone who knew it. He immediately began to execute the plan I gave him and we continually tweaked it over the months and years ahead to produce massive success. In a very short time he retired from his previous company and today has one of the largest marketing networks in the world.

That's the power of an accurate Action Blueprint!

Creating a (Flexible) Action Blueprint

What we're going to do is create a definite plan for attaining your Ultimate Goal. Don't worry if it's not perfect; you can always correct it along the way. The main thing is, you have an Action Blueprint and you put it into practice immediately, whether you're ready or not.

Goals are written in concrete, plans are written in sand. Many times you'll have to adjust your plan along the way. This is natural and part of life; so don't worry about having to make adjustments.

Flexibility is a key aspect in life; you see what doesn't work and you adjust your course. Another one of my mentors is author, speaker and trainer, Brian Tracy. Brian is a world-renowned expert on setting and achieving goals. Although Brian is a big proponent of creating accurate action plans to achieve your goals, he also teaches that flexibility is one of the keys to effective planning. In his book, *Flight Plan-The Real Secret to Success,* he explains that life is like an airplane journey. From the time you take off you will be off course 99% of the time just like an airplane is. The purpose and role of the pilot and the avionics is to continually bring the plane back on course, so that it arrives on schedule at its destination. It only needs to be precisely on course when it lands, right?

It's the same thing with us; the destination must be crystal clear with a time and date for arrival. We must have a plan so we don't stray too far off course, but we can keep correcting along the way.

In order to help build your faith and inspire you to do this process, let me tell you a true story that demonstrates that your plan doesn't have to be perfect. It will be modified along the way as long as you have a big dream and take action while being flexible. The only absolute requirements are a big dream that moves you and the consistent action you must take to make it a reality.

The story is about the start of Microsoft, one of the world's most powerful and valuable corporations.

In December of 1974, a young Paul Allen bought a copy of *Popular Mechanics*, which had a picture on the cover of the revolutionary new microcomputer kit, the MITS Altair 8080. The Altair 8080 had 8 kilobytes of memory (compared to 1 Gigabyte or more in most PCs today) but no operating software. Allen convinced Bill Gates that they should start a company and develop a language for the simple machine.

Gates was attending Harvard and trying to convince Allen to try to land a programmer job at Honeywell so they could continue work on their dreams for a software company. Gates and Allen called the founder of MITS and promised an Altair program before they had even written it. The two rushed to a mainframe computer at Harvard, meant to be used for student projects, not for commercial work, and expropriated it for their project.

Since they didn't have an Altair 8080 computer, they had to figure out how it functioned from the magazine article and then simulate it on the Harvard mainframe. Can you imagine this? These two gutsy guys promised to deliver a program they hadn't written for a computer they didn't even have.

So what did they do? They took massive action to make their dream a reality! They went to work writing code like maniacs in Bill's dorm room. By March of 1975, they had written the program. Paul Allen then flew to Albuquerque to demonstrate it.

Remember, they wrote the program without even being able to test it on the actual computer. They weren't totally sure it would work.

They acted on faith, faith in their dreams, faith in their abilities and knowledge and faith in their actions. That program was called BASIC and it became the industry standard for the next six years.

Gates dropped out of Harvard, he and Allen started MicroSoft Corporation and the rest is history. Microsoft was born by the massive actions of two driven guys with a huge dream—creating something that didn't exist at the time they promised to deliver it.

How's that for producing phenomenal results with a big dream, a flexible action blueprint that changes as needed, and massive action on the dream? The whole story of Microsoft shows (and continues to do so even today) how clarity of purpose and consistent action with flexibility of plans is the key to their success. And it's the key to your success too!

There are numerous success stories of great people throughout history creating their own reality and destinies by taking massive action on their dreams while staying flexible with their action plans, from the founders of Google, Sergey Brin and Larry Page, to one of the best movie directors of all time, Steven Spielberg. In every industry, whether high tech or Hollywood, people are inventing, innovating and creating a better world. Let's do the same for you right now. Let's begin to take the actions that will create the future of your dreams.

Build on a Solid Foundation

I give you this pep talk because usually after people stretch themselves and create a huge compelling goal they freak out and ask themselves… How am I ever going to attain such a big goal? It has us fired up but at the same time it makes us kind of anxious.

I want you to know that we live in an abundant world full of information and knowledge and it's never been easier to obtain it. If you haven't noticed yet, there's something called the Internet with a tool called Google where you can find anything at all that you want to know.

If your Ultimate Goal is in the business or financial area of your life, realize that your business or career is part of an industry or profession where there's a great probability that somebody has already done what you want to do or achieved the level of success, income or net-worth that you desire.

If your Ultimate Goal is in the relationship area of your life, somebody has developed the relationships that you desire to have full of love, romance, respect, adventure, fun and joy.

If your Ultimate Goal is in the emotional area, somebody lives daily in the emotional states that you desire to experience be it love, peace, harmony, courage, confidence, success, wealth, happiness, creativity, mastery or joy.

If it's in the physical area, someone has gotten healed of that disease you are fighting off in a holistic manner. Someone has lost the amount of weight that you want to lose. Someone has done the type of exercise that you need to do to get into top shape, has learned to eat correctly to not only lose weight but also be healthy and full of energy and vitality.

All you have to do is find the person who already is, does, has or gives what you desire and make them your mentor, in other words, model them. Think and do what they do and you will have the same results.

Today's world is full of experts in all areas ready to teach you to get the results you want. I am part of an organization called *The Experts Industry Association*. Our members are dedicated to educating and training people worldwide to achieve the success they desire in whatever area they can imagine. We have multi-millionaire business people, experts in on-line marketing, direct marketing, and network marketing. We have doctors, chiropractors, nutritionists, physical trainers, experts in neuroscience, quantum physics, philosophy, spirituality, psychologists, relationships, everything that you can imagine and even more.

Ladies and gentlemen, today we live in the era of transformation. It is no longer the information age. We have entered into a time where the knowledge and wisdom of the world is available to anyone who seeks and has ears to hear. There are people dedicated to this whose passion and mission in life is this. I know this beyond a doubt because I am one of them and I can show you how to transform any area of your life.

Although I love to innovate I've learned over the years to be practical first. I've learned to build my foundation on solid rock instead of sand. Let's do this for you too and start creating your action plan on the easiest path possible. So my first question to you is, who in your business or industry has the success you want? Do they have a systematic program for people to follow? Do they have seminars or events where you can go and learn? Do they have an on-line or physical program that teaches you a framework or systematic action process you can follow? If there is, buy it, learn it and follow it to produce your results.

Find the best in your profession or industry and use their plan of action. The same goes for health and wellness, weight loss, relationship excellence and emotional well-being. Find the expert who can show you their action blueprint and follow it. Before you innovate use what has already been proven to work. Then once you have results you can improve it if you want.

If you can't find anything in your field I have a generic process that's applicable to any area and you're going to learn it right now in this book. If you want to really master it you can register for my **Unlimited Success Academy** (http://unlimitedsuccessacademy.com) online course or live event where you can take your training to a much higher level than you possibly can in any book because I can guide you more thoroughly.

If you don't have a plan of action to follow, created by someone who has the results you want or seek, let me teach you a super effective process.

The human imagination is a very powerful tool. It is the power that Infinite Intelligence has given us to create our own life according to our likes. If you are able to imagine your dream, your Ultimate Goal accomplished (which you have already done), you can take things to whole new level. You can use your imagination to help you create an effective plan of action.

Right now, look at your Ultimate Goal and really connect emotionally with your reasons for achieving it.

See It As Already Done

The way I teach my students to create their Action Blueprint is to go to the end, to the point where they've already achieved their Ultimate Goal and imagine it's already done. Visualize your Ultimate Goal achieved and feel like it's already done; you already are that person, doing and having what you desired. Now, how did you get there? Just as you imagined being there, you can also imagine how you got there. This way, you are using the unlimited power of Infinite Intelligence to guide you.

Think about the achievement point of your Ultimate Goal and see, hear and feel in your imagination:

- What was your official date of achievement?
- Who are you? What is your life like?
- How do you think?
- How did you think to get here?
- What do you believe?
- What did you believe to get here?
- How do you act?
- How did you act to get here?
- Who did you partner with to get here?
- Who was your team that helped you get here?
- What specifically did you do to get here?

Take a few moments to close your eyes and really imagine having achieved this Ultimate Goal and <u>knowing how you got here</u>, the plan you followed. With this level of motivation, sit down, refocus and write your plan of action, your Action Blueprint, including what value you intend to give and/or what you intend to do in order to achieve it.

If you have any doubts you can always borrow a plan from someone who has already achieved what you want and you can model them and their plan. The most important thing is for you to get started right now with yours and you can refine it later.

Here, I'll let you borrow my plan for inspiration. I set my Ultimate Goal to become a millionaire in 1986 and I've shared with you my reasons why. With a little humility, I'm showing you my initial plan. You'll see it doesn't have to be perfect. Today, I look back on this and am quite amused by the simplistic nature of it, but it motivated me and guided me back then.

My Ultimate Goal: I am totally committed to being a millionaire by August 1, 1988.

My Action Blueprint:

1. To achieve this goal I will hit the <u>Diamond</u> achievement level in my business helping <u>six</u> of my group leaders attain their goals.

2. I will recruit 20 to 30 personal leaders and help the most committed six to 10 achieve their goals.

3. I will outwork everybody.

4. I will do and teach a building pattern that incorporates twice as much productive activity as is currently being taught.

5. I will do over 30 group business presentations per month.

6. I will make 10 recruiting calls per day whether for personal recruits or their prospects.

7. I will make third party calls for my new recruits and teach my leaders to do the same for their organizations.

8. I will lead by example and get my leaders duplicating the intensity of my actions.

9. I will create such momentum that my whole organization will be pulled into a vacuum that drives them to success.

10. My mottoes are: The speed of the leader determines the speed of the group. If it's to be it's up to me. Some

will, some won't, so what…Next! What I do speaks so loudly that what I say you cannot hear. The more people I help get what they want the more I get what I want. Therefore my focus is to help thousands of people become financially free!

As basic as this was, it drove me to accomplish my Ultimate Goal and then some. Even though my plan wasn't perfect, and I did modify it along the way many times, the action it created and the focus on results took me much further than the accuracy of the plan itself. The first house I bought after achieving my goal was 8,000 square feet on three acres (instead of 5,000 sq. ft. on two acres), the clothes and jewelry were way more than we imagined. Shortly thereafter I was flying first class on all of my trips and staying in the most luxurious hotel suites around the world. We had a live-in nanny and homeschooled our daughters all the way until junior high school when they decided they wanted to go to "real school." I was able to give way more than $100,000 to charity annually including over $250,000 in one year to two of my favorite charities in Mexico, which rescued, fed, clothed and educated abandoned children, in addition to the six-figure donations to my church. With the momentum started in this process, I helped over 70 people become millionaires and thousands become financially free.

To give you a head start on your Action Blueprint, here is a tool that I use to this day. The key is to focus on taking consistent action daily that will move you in the direction of your desired outcome. Decide that you will write down and take at least five actions that will move you closer to your desired outcome, every single day. While I specify today in each action step of *My Daily Five* they should be modified as needed daily in order to achieve your goals.

My Daily Five

1. What are the most important actions I must take today?

_____

_____

_____

2. Who are the most important people to motivate, manage or collaborate with today?

_____

_____

_____

3. What is the most important resource I can use today?

_____

_____

_____

4. What is/are the most important belief(s) I need to have and focus on today?

_____

_____

_____

5. What will I do to hold myself and my team accountable today?

_____

_____

_____

As soon as you're done with this exercise, take the first action immediately. Do not delay. Who can you call? What meeting can you set up? Do not put it off for later. **Do It Now!** Develop that habit. Determine that the only thing you're going to procrastinate in life from now on is procrastination.

Welcome back! Are you excited? I'm excited for you! Having done this several times in my life, I know how it feels. I know it can sometimes be scary, but trust me. If you stay focused on your Ultimate Goal, you'll achieve it and then some, and you'll be hooked on this process. You will be directing your focus and building the life of your dreams.

I cannot stress this enough to you. You direct your thoughts and your mind and you create your destiny because everything — your decisions, actions, habits, abilities, results in life — will all be determined by your thoughts and your thoughts will be determined by your focus.

You'll also begin to look at problems in a more detached manner. You'll see the opportunities they bring can actually help you achieve your Ultimate Goal even faster or bigger than you imagined.

Read your Ultimate Goal statement and visualize yourself having accomplished it every day, when you wake up in the morning and again before going to sleep at night. Associate yourself to your Ultimate Goal as often as possible.

As you do this daily, you'll get really good at it. You'll make a movie out of it in your mind and as you perfect it, you'll begin to attract the people, circumstances and events necessary to making it a reality in the physical realm. Also, the more you do this, the easier you'll find it to maintain your focus on what you want and not on what you don't want.

As we close this section, allow your mind to contemplate and grasp the significance of these immortal lines of James Allen from the book, *As A Man Thinketh*:

The dreamers are the saviors of the world. As the visible world is sustained by the invisible, so humanity through all its trials and mistakes and suffering, is nourished by the beautiful visions of its solitary dreamers.

Humanity cannot forget its dreamers; it cannot let their ideals fade and die. It lives in them; it knows them as the realities, which it shall one day see and know.

The vision that you glorify in your mind, the ideal that you enthrone in your heart—this you will build your life by, and this you will become.

Chapter 11

STEP SEVEN: TAKE INSPIRED ACTION

Inspiration without Action is merely entertainment. Act on your Inspiration today.

—Mary Morrissey

Lights, Camera, INSPIR-ACTION

This chapter is all about taking action... massive, consistent, *inspired* action towards achieving your desired outcomes.

In all actuality, directing your focus is deciding what to pay attention to and then *taking the action* of directing your attention. Rejecting negative influences or inaccurate information is also making a decision and is also *taking an action.*

Physical action is actually the harvesting part in the creative process. The real creation happens in the mind through mental action. Imagination is the power to create and thought is creative energy, so *thought is the most potent action* that you can take and it always precedes physical action! You see, it's like growing crops. You take the seed, which is the idea or desire, and you plant it in the ground, which is the subconscious, by imagining what you desire. Then you water it and fertilize it by maintaining your focus on it and imagining with strong feeling that your desire is already achieved. This is how you take care of the crop. It grows and matures in consciousness and when it is ready to harvest, you thrust in the sickle (physical action) and you begin to harvest.

That is really what action is. Very few people get it because they've worked at jobs where they do specific functions or tasks that are part of the overall whole. They don't see the full picture, someone else conceived it through their mental action and they've only been given a portion of the entirety to perform, therefore, they think that action is the key to creating when it is actually the harvesting step.

At the end of the day, we're living in a physical world and what we're striving to manifest are physical things. The action part is actually collecting what belongs to you already because you've created it mentally through imagination, whether intentionally or unintentionally.

If you're not motivated to take action, the first thing you must do is see if your reason or motive is big enough and compelling enough to move you to take action. *If you have powerless dreams and goals, you will not be driven to take action, furthermore, your fears will actually <u>prevent</u> you from taking action.*

Can't See Dreams and Problems at the Same Time

Focus is the ultimate power given to us to create our reality. It can change the way you think and feel in an instant. It is nothing more than the act of directing your conscious attention towards something like a thought, person, situation, dream, goal, desire, fear, worry, feeling or emotion. It is also the meaning you give to whatever you're paying attention to. Think of focusing the lens of a camera and zooming in on something.

You can't see your dreams and your problems at the same time so whatever you focus on is what you get. If you focus on the problem your imagination magnifies it and it grows bigger, more ominous and more overpowering, so you feel overwhelmed, frustrated, depressed and unhappy. This causes you to vibrate at a negative, low frequency, which attracts more of the people, events and conditions that match that low, negative frequency. You have in essence attracted more of the same thing (your problem).

Conversely, if you direct your focus toward your dreams and goals, you don't see the problems. You see what you desire and, if you zoom in on it, your imagination makes it bigger and brighter and you'll begin to feel excitement, expectation, enthusiasm, passion, happiness, success and fun. This causes you to vibrate at a positive, high frequency, which attracts more of the people, events and conditions that match that high positive frequency. You have purposely attracted your dreams!

Always remember…where attention goes, energy flows!

If you think about it, every great success, every great fortune that was ever created, came as a result of solving a problem.

The bigger the problem, the better the solution, the greater the reward!

The power of focus is so important that it's the only thing our Creator gave us absolute power to control in our lives. It is the <u>vehicle</u> through which we control our own minds. It is also the vehicle through which we can direct our imagination to influence our subconscious mind, which is the foundation of this whole book!

Another of my mentors is speaker, consultant, and author of, *The Psychology of Winning*, Dr. Denis Waitley. I met Denis at an event over 20 years ago and subsequently brought him in to speak numerous times to my marketing organizations at my live conventions. One thing he always said in his talks was, "In life you'll never, ever, ever get what you want… (long pause for effect), you'll only get what you expect!" Then he'd go on to explain that you expect the things you constantly maintain your focus on. I couldn't agree more and Denis has had a great impact on the success I've enjoyed throughout my career.

One of my favorite things to do is go boating and as I achieved my success I was able to afford to take it up as my hobby. I attributed my success to my power of focus so much that the two yachts I've owned in my life I named FOCUS and FOCUS II. But understand, this focusing ability did not come naturally to me, as I get distracted by the issues of life as much as the next guy. I had to develop this ability through constant practice.

The New Millionaire

What you do speaks so loudly that I cannot hear what you say.
—Ralph Waldo Emerson

I told you in Step Three (Chapter 7) I'd finish the story on how I became a millionaire, so here it is. At that (now familiar) leadership seminar I made the decision to become a millionaire in 28 months. I went back home and immediately started negotiating with my partners to buy my share of the energy management business so I could build my marketing network full time. I negotiated a sale within a couple of weeks and set off after my dream.

I totally committed to overcoming all of my limitations by outworking everybody and holding myself to a higher standard than anyone expected of me. Since leadership is by example in my business, my leaders and even the newer recruits quickly followed my lead and started duplicating my actions and intensity level. Becoming a millionaire became my burning desire. I focused on it constantly as I confidently searched for the right ambitious people with a dream who wanted to work with me. Because of my focus, dedication and intensity of activity, I found some great people and created my own breaks.

I literally attracted the right people to me to achieve my goal. The harder I worked, the luckier I got, although it didn't feel like hard work because I was doing what I loved to do and doing it with passion. I developed the mindset that was totally congruent with who I was committed to being and the beliefs that supported it. And mind you, at this time, I really didn't fully understand all the principles.

I was only modeling several people who had the results I desired so my focus was on being a millionaire. I imagined myself being and acting like them. I imagined my business growing as fast and even faster than theirs. I did this religiously every morning upon waking up, every night before falling asleep, and as many times as I could throughout my day. I imagined all of this so much in the quiet moments that I found myself driving to meetings in my car imagining myself giving speeches to packed auditoriums and coliseums teaching how I had succeeded and the principles of success.

It became both amusing and exciting to me that I could drive for an hour or two all the while imagining myself as a successful entrepreneur giving speeches on success for the entire time with my eyes still open. I literally ate, slept and breathed being a millionaire in every moment and began to act like one not just in my mind but also consistently in every waking moment. I acted on my Action Blueprint and continually strove to even outperform myself. I became a massive action machine and 28 months later, as you already know by now, the achievement of my dream culminated with that keynote speech I had envisioned so many times before to a packed house of 15,000+ people. That is the power of massive action and the proper use of the Be It principle, which you will learn in the next step!

I want to make sure you understand that I am not a proponent of delusive thinking and behavior. This book is not only about positive thinking and affirmations; we are working with the laws and principles of the universe. Through my story you have just witnessed that once you have a clearly defined Ultimate Goal and an Action Blueprint, then massive inspired action is the natural consequence and what is required to make it happen!

I attribute my high standards and extraordinary work ethic to my father. When I was growing up, my parents worked very hard and sacrificed personal luxuries in order for my sisters and I to get a good education and be well prepared for life. Because of that I had to sacrifice personal luxuries also, unless I was willing to work for them. When my friends got the cool 10-speed bikes and I was still riding my un-cool banana seat bike, I asked my dad for a 10-speed.

He said we couldn't afford it, but that if I cut the lawn at our house every week then he'd lend me our lawnmower so I could go out and cut some of our neighbors' lawns to make money. I also got the idea to upsell my lawn-mowing customers and got them to pay me to wash their cars, too.

When I went to high school and wanted the cool Nik-Nik shirts and Wayfarer jeans, my dad said he'd provide the regular clothes I needed for school and church, but I had to work for the rest. By the way, by this point my three sisters and I were all attending private schools. Obviously, when I wanted a car I already knew what the answer would be, so I was prepared in advance. I worked all throughout the year, even during football season where I was the starting running back for our team, in order to have what I wanted and buy my first car. Back then I resented my dad a bit for making me work, but today I am ever so grateful because I learned to be self-sufficient and make things happen in my own life. Today my family and I enjoy financial freedom and a lifestyle that few people have due to the focus and work ethic that I learned growing up. Thanks, Dad!

Proof of Inspired Action

Superstar and entrepreneur, Will Smith, also developed a very strong work ethic from early in his youth. His movies have now grossed over $5 billion, but before he became the maven that he is now, it was his father who set the foundation for a belief system to which he attributes his success.

Smith has said, "Where I excel is I have a ridiculous, sickening work ethic. While the other guy is eating I'm working, while the other guy is sleeping, I'm working. I will not be outworked period. You might have more talent than me, be smarter than me, but if we get on a treadmill together either you're going to get off before me or I'm going to die. Success is strictly based on hustle. It's about outworking everyone. The guy who is willing to hustle the most is the guy that's going to win."

Will Smith is a prime example of the Inspired Action principle!

You must continually take massive positive action, both mental as well as physical action daily, in the direction of your desired outcomes. This is accurate thinking.

Accurate Thinking

Accurate thinking is the byproduct of living your life according to Universal Principles, as opposed to prior conditioning. Remember that your initial thought habits and thinking patterns came from your physical heredity or your ancestry. The way your family thought and their family thought and their family thought was all passed along to you.

Most people think and act a certain way due to family influence or social conditioning and suffer tremendously from inaccurate thinking. How can it be otherwise if others determined most of your thinking and the majority of those others are broke, frustrated and unhappy?

To think accurately you must always do five things:

1. Stay focused on your dreams and goals and ask yourself if what you're thinking about right now is getting you closer to your ideal life.
2. Separate fact from opinions, hearsay, gossip, rumor and hypothesis.

3. Separate facts into two categories — important and unimportant.
4. Ask yourself what beliefs, feelings or emotions are driving this thinking and are they serving you?
5. What is the principle-based way to think about this? Then think in the principle-based way!

You cannot accept or act upon any opinion given to you that is not based on facts or principles. You cannot allow negative emotions, feelings or limiting beliefs to direct your thinking. You cannot permit anyone to do your thinking for you. Realize that you're constantly being bombarded by other people trying to suck you into their problems, agendas and interests. If you allow those distractions you are not in control of your life.

Your decisions and actions should always be based upon Universal Principles and be congruent with your dreams and goals. And, while we're on the topic of accurate thinking, there are three critical habits that I want to share.

Critical Habit #1: *Control your mind and thoughts!*
Take full and complete <u>possession</u> of your own mind and attitude. You direct your life on purpose by directing your own mind and thoughts. It is exactly what we are working on together throughout this entire book!

Critical Habit #2: *Live in the positive emotions that empower you to create on purpose and release any negative emotion that comes up consistently.*
Make sure you live your life in the emotional states you value most. By releasing negative emotions and directing <u>your focus</u> continually

to your dreams and goals, you will begin to give empowering meaning to all events and circumstances.

Critical Habit #3: *Take massive inspired action daily in order to achieve your dreams and goals!*
You have defined many times (and in various ways) throughout this book what it is you desire in your life, gaining greater clarity every step along the way, leading to your Ultimate Goal and creating an Action Blueprint to achieve it.

You've learned a powerful strategy to remain clear and aligned in every moment and now I'm going to teach you a very important strategy in order for you to act with confidence and power at will!

The Law of Reversibility

There is an interesting principle called the Law of Reversibility, which basically states that all transformations of force are reversible. If heat can produce mechanical motion, then mechanical motion can produce heat. If electricity can be produced by friction, then friction can be produced by electricity.

Therefore, if a certain emotion can make you act a certain way then acting that way can also generate the same emotion. That's what we mean by emotion is created by motion!

The really useful thing about this principle is that if you use the form and function of your body (physiology) correctly, you can generate the emotions or feelings you desire to experience and get yourself to take appropriate action in the moment.

If I told you there was a very depressed person outside your door right now, could you describe the person to me? Of course you could. His shoulders would be drooping, his head hanging, eyes looking down. You could also guess that he was overwhelmed by his problems.

Well, how do we know all of this? Because we've seen it and even experienced it ourselves many times and our subconscious knows all of it.

If I told you there was a very enthusiastic and confident person outside your door right now, could you tell me what she looks like? Of course you could! She's standing tall, chest up, shoulders back, head held high, eyes focused and confident, smiling. Right?

See, you know that, too, but let me tell you how valuable this is. If you know how this works, you can pull it off whenever you want. Right now where you are, stand up. Don't put the book down! Keep reading while you stand.

Now, think about something you really dislike doing, something you're afraid of, something you're so bad at that when anyone asks you to do it, you panic and feel awful. Think about it and pretend I'm asking you to do that thing right now. How do you feel, how are you standing, what's your posture, how are you breathing, what's the position of your head, what's going through your head? 'Oh no, I don't want to do this.' See how that feels?

Next, think of something you love to do, something you're great at, something you do so well that you have all the confidence in the world doing it. Stand how you would stand if you were anticipating actually going and doing it right now.

How's your posture, your breathing, your facial expression, head position, etc.?

You're fired up, head high, shoulders back, chest out, breathing strong, smiling and thinking good thoughts! Isn't it amazing?

You know exactly how do to this already. You can get yourself in positive emotional states at will; *you know how to do this.*

Isn't it interesting that you already know how to put yourself in positive and negative postures? Practice a few times going from the stance of thinking about that thing you hate to do and aren't good at (feel how it feels) to the totally confident stance of what you love to do and are great at (feel how that feels). Jump back and forth between the two states several times right now. Feel the states in your body and snap right into the physiology and feelings corresponding to each state until you can turn on the empowering state at will.

Practice this technique at least <u>10 times</u> today and each day <u>for one week</u> so you can get really good at going from a negative state to a positive state. Then, when something happens to put you in a negative state, you can immediately refocus your thoughts by focusing on what you love to do and feel confident doing and snap into a positive state.

Understand that you can do this any time you want, because you are in charge. It's your body; it's your physiology and your mind! You now have the tools to turn on feelings of confidence and power at will and turn yourself into a human dynamo.

Power Up with Your Power Trigger

Now that you know how to snap yourself into a state of confidence with the previous exercise let's take it one step further. Let's create a physical trigger that can turn on that confidence at will just like flipping a switch to turn on a powerful generator. Wouldn't that be useful?

Read the instructions first and then do the exercise. What I want you to do is once again imagine you are going to do the thing you love to do, are good at and feel total confidence doing. Then close your eyes and imagine you are doing it and doing it better than you ever have before. When you are at the peak level of feeling, excitement, exuberance, joy and really feeling your power and confidence, make a fist with your right hand, squeeze it tight and say with emotion, "My Power."

Repeat this process <u>10 times</u>, each time trying to increase how well you do the thing you are confident doing, in your imagination and at the same time feeling increased levels of excitement, confidence and joy and truly feeling your power and confidence increasing as you make a tight fist with your right hand and say with high emotion, "My Power!" You should now be able to close your fist and say, "My Power," and bring back the feeling of confidence and power.

If you will practice this exercise at least <u>10 times</u> more today and then <u>10 times per day for the next week</u>, you will be able to turn on your feelings of confidence and power at will simply by using your Power Trigger. This is because the way we human beings are wired, whenever we consistently associate a highly emotional mental stimulus with a distinct physiological stimulus the two get tied together. Then any time you fire the physical stimulus, which I call a trigger, you also fire off the emotional and mental associations that you paired with it. When I use my Power Trigger I instantaneously go into a powerful and confident state at will, no matter what the circumstances might be, and you can too. All it takes is practice. Repetition is the mother of skill!

Your Inspired Action Tools

Take the First Step

If your dream is compelling but you're still not taking consistent action, the next question to ask yourself is, 'What do I fear?' What pain are you trying to avoid? Again, this is where the previous exercises we did become so valuable.

You can now check and see if your identity or beliefs are in conflict or you need to release an emotional scar or deep-seated fear that you might not be aware of consciously in order to avert self-sabotage and empower yourself to take action. You now have the tools to change limiting beliefs and release negative feelings, emotions and memories with some of the clearing techniques you've learned.

Remember, I had an insane fear of speaking in public when I started out and learned to feel the fear and take action anyway because action cures fear.

An old Chinese proverb states: The journey of a thousand miles begins with the first step. Take the first step, even if you're scared to death. However, with what you've learned in this book so far, you know to first release and re-align and then act. As I've told people for years, you can't wait for all the lights to turn green before you begin or you'll never get anywhere.

Affirm-Actions

Using affirmations is an action in and of itself. Remember the affirmation, "I am whole, perfect, strong, powerful, loving, harmonious, prosperous and happy." Use that often, especially in the morning when you wake up and at night before going to sleep.

Get centered with the truth. Aligning yourself is the most important action that you can take because you connect with the true power within you, which leads to massive *inspired* action. That still, small voice within, which is your higher self, gives you hunches and feelings that lead to your taking spontaneous correct action (inspiration = in-

Spirit-action). And that is what you want to do, act from a point of power. You never want to act out of fear, anxiety or desperation, because the results are never right. Always act from a state of power and confidence!

Go talk to somebody on a sales call with fear that you are not going to get the sale and you won't get the sale. Go talk to a prospect with fear of lack, thinking, 'I've got to close this sale because if not I don't know how I'm going to pay the rent,' and you're going to project that and not make the sale.

Always clear and align first using the Alignment Strategy in Step Five (Chapter 9) before going in, then use your Power Trigger to act with total confidence and then your actions will lead to positive results.

Act *from* the feeling of the desire fulfilled. Once you start taking action on your dreams and goals, you'll gain momentum and naturally focus on them automatically.

Decide and Act

In life, not making a decision *is making a decision* and not taking action *is taking action*. However, those are the worst decisions and actions you could possibly take. Making no decision and taking no action put you at the mercy of those people around you who are making decisions and taking actions.

Do you want to be subservient to someone else who doesn't have your dreams and desires as their number one priority? Do you want to lead your life according to the desires of other people around you who have their own agenda? The worst thing you can do in life is relinquish the right to the most important gifts our Creator gave us, the right to decide and take action towards what *we* desire in life.

By now, through the exercises and assignments you've done, you have begun to adjust your mindset and its corresponding subconscious beliefs to one that serves you, instead of one that betrays and sabotages you continually.

In the last chapter you created a daily Action Blueprint to achieve your desired results. That plan will become the central point to directing your action on a daily basis. The key to your success and the timeframe for achieving it will be how consistently you focus on your desired outcomes and execute your Action Blueprint, maintaining flexibility and enhancing your plan along the way!

Be flexible because flexibility = power. And in the next step I'll share with you the secret of secrets.

Chapter 12

STEP EIGHT: BE IT

As a man thinks in his heart so is he.

—**Proverbs 23:7**

Be to Have

Now we've come to the single most important chapter in the entire book. We've been alluding to this principle all along and if you've been paying attention, you've caught it already. In reality, this is where the rubber meets the road and the secret of all success and achievement is revealed. In short: **The secret of doing, having and giving is <u>Being</u>.**

As you've seen in previous steps, all the wisdom literature states in one way or another that creation is about Infinite Intelligence becoming physical form. When we read that we were made in the image and likeness of God that means we are made of the same substance, which is infinitely intelligent energy. Take the image and expand it a bit and you get imagining or imagination, which is the beginning of any creative process and produces the physical form or likeness of the image held in the mind. That is how Infinite Intelligence creates, by imagining Itself being and then becoming the thing it desires or intends. After all, it is omnipresent, which simply means It is everywhere and is <u>everything</u>. This is what is meant by the verse, I Am that (the thing desired)—I Am (it now!).

How do we use this principle in our lives to create whatever we desire? It's quite simple... the key is to *Be It*!

Thought leader, Neville Goddard, in his powerful book, *The Power of Awareness,* states, "By creating an ideal in your mental sphere and assuming you are already that ideal you identify with it and transform into its image (thinking <u>from</u> the ideal instead of thinking <u>of</u> it). Every state is already there as 'mere possibilities' as long as we think <u>of</u> them but as overpoweringly real when we think <u>from</u> them."

In many interviews and videos on YouTube, award-winning actor Jim Carrey has talked about his early career when he was broke and working towards his big break. He told the story of how every night he drove through Mulholland Drive in Los Angeles and visualized having directors interested in him, telling him they liked his work. One day he wrote himself a check for $10 million dollars for acting services rendered and dated it Thanksgiving 1995. He carried that check in his wallet and just before Thanksgiving 1995, he found out he was going to make $10 million dollars for his movie, *Dumb and Dumber*. Today Jim says, "I have an insane belief in my own ability to manifest things. I believe we are creators. I believe we create with every thought, with every word."

He continually acted as if he was a star, keeping his focus and working diligently on his dream. Jim Carrey used the Be It principle to go from starving actor to one of the highest paid actors in Hollywood.

American swimmer and world record holder Michael Phelps is the most decorated Olympian of all time, with a total of 22 medals, and he epitomizes the power of the Be It principle. In the 2008 Beijing Games, Phelps won eight medals and took the record for the most first-place finishes at any single Olympic Games. In the 2012 Summer Olympics in London, Phelps won four gold and two silver medals, making him the most successful athlete of the Games yet again.

Here is this man, who dominates his sport and is an inspiration to people around the world, and he credits his success just as much to his mental game as to the physical. His coach, Bob Bowman has said, "He's the best I've ever seen and maybe the best ever in terms of visualization. He will see exactly the perfect race. He will see it like he is in the stands and he'll see it like he's in the water."

Point A to Point B

In the beginning of this book we talked about where you are in your life and called it Point A. Then we identified that you really don't want to be at Point A. You actually are dissatisfied with Point A, so you'd like to be some place else. We called that Point B.

Point B is everything that you desire in the specific areas that you would like to change in your life. That's your financial picture, your physical picture, your relationship picture, emotional picture, or all of it.

The more precision you utilize in defining Point B, the clearer picture you have of it, the easier it is to attain Point B. The more reasons or benefits you have for attaining Point B for yourself or your loved ones, the more power your vision generates and the easier you will attain it.

In your imagination you can cross over the bridge from where you are at Point A to where you'd like to be at Point B and see yourself already being that Point B person. You can discover how that Point B person thinks. You can see how that Point B person perceives the world around him or her.

What does that Point B person believe and how does he or she exercise that belief? How does that Point B person act? How does he perceive himself? How does she perceive other people? How does he perceive the world? The government, economy, political scene? How does that person see and perceive everything around her in order to have that life, to have that specific result, the one that you're looking for?

If you can assume the consciousness of already Being It, if you can assume the state of mind, the way of thinking, the way of believing, the way of processing information. If you can assume that you already are that person, that you already have those things that you desire to have, including the lifestyle, the relationships, the body, the emotional states. If you can <u>imagine</u>, which doesn't just mean visualize, it means <u>feeling</u> that you <u>are</u> already it, seeing the world <u>from</u> that state of consciousness, acting as if you're already that person, then you will have it now.

The difference between visualizing and Being It is this: When you visualize, you are seeing yourself in a movie, watching yourself do things, just like when you see a video of yourself. Being It is when you are in the movie and star of it… you <u>are</u> it! You are seeing the world <u>from</u> your own inner eyes, the version of you that already is it, does it and has it. You are seeing, hearing, feeling as though you already <u>are</u>.

You have assumed the consciousness, the mindset, the belief system, the thinking of the person who already is it, does it and has it.

When you come back across the bridge from that Point B to where you are and you bring the consciousness with you of that Point B person, that Point B lifestyle, that Point B mindset back to your Point A, and you start living, acting, thinking, processing, believing and being that Point B person, you will produce your desired results at a speed that will shock and surprise you.

"As you believe, it is done unto you." (Matt. 9:29)

I used to hear the phrase, "Fake it 'til you make it," from some of my first mentors. This may sound a little hokey to some people because they think of faking it as a falsity, right? While today I prefer to say, "Faith it 'til you make it," which is actually more accurate, many people have used faking it to achieve greater levels of success than they ever could have otherwise. Keep in mind, as I've stated previously, even if what you believe is not true, the Law of Belief will produce it just as readily as a true fact.

Many people say, "I'll believe it when I see it." That's why they never achieve anything. They only see it when someone else who had the vision already created it. The reality of life is that, "When you believe it, you'll see it."

Now is not the time to be realistic. You don't want to settle for mediocre. You want phenomenal. Decide that you are a success. Act in total faith that it is <u>done</u>! This is the power of Be It and this is the greatest secret of all. If there was only one principle you could use to produce whatever results you wanted in life with the assurance that it would happen, it would be this one. If you live this principle, everything else is commentary. This is the key to realizing all of your dreams and desires.

Ideal Life Story

Last year at an Experts Industry Association event, I met an incredible lady, international speaker, best selling author of *Building Your Field of Dreams*, and empowerment specialist, Mary Morrissey, and immediately resonated with her. Being the eternal student that I am, I signed up for one of her courses called Quantum Leap. Interestingly, one of the very first exercises she has her students do is write a very detailed Vision Statement. She states that the vision you are holding in your mind must always be clearer, larger and more magnificent than the conditions or circumstances in which you presently find yourself. In writing your vision ask yourself first and foremost, 'What would I love?' Be specific. Paint the picture of the life you would love to live, exactly as you desire it to be. Be descriptive and five-sensorize it. How does it feel, taste, look, sound and smell? Describe the life you would absolutely LOVE living in the four key domains of life, your health, relationships, career or creative expression, and your time and money freedom.

We've done a lot of that leg work already and what we're going to do right now is merge all of the exercises you've done so far into a story that expresses in vivid detail what your life is like after having accomplished all of your highest dreams and goals. You are going to paint the picture of the life you would absolutely LOVE to be living. In this process you will learn how to consistently direct your focus in a systematic manner in order to make it real. This is one of the most fun and compelling exercises you will ever do and one that will pay huge dividends for the rest of your life!

Let your imagination run wild, let go and have fun with this!

Since you are now the person that you desire to be, you have everything that you desire to have, you are doing everything that you desire to do, and you are giving everything you desire to give, what is your life like? Describe it in detail. This is like going to the end of the movie when the hero or heroine has already achieved the goal, has already overcome all the obstacles and accomplished their objective. They've gotten the prize, they are living happily ever after or riding off into the sunset. What does that mean for you?

What is it like? What is that lifestyle for you and your loved ones? Describe it in ultimate detail. Where do you live? Is your house by the ocean, a lake or in the mountains? Describe the house in full detail. What type of house is it? Is it Mediterranean? Is it Tudor? Is it colonial? What does it look like? How are you feeling, surrounded by all this beauty? How happy and fulfilled are your loved ones?

Walk around inside the house. What does your master bedroom look like? What kind of window treatments do you have? What does the kitchen look like? What does the family room look like? Look out the window, what's outside? Is there a balcony? What's beyond the balcony? Is there a swimming pool, and if so what does it look like? What's the landscaping, the environment look like? If it's on the ocean, describe its sounds, sights and feelings in detail. If it's on a lake or mountain, do the same thing.

What type of art is in your house, what décor, what furnishings? If you go into the garage, what's in it? How many vehicles are parked in it? What are the automobiles that you have there? What make, model and color are they, along with their pertinent characteristics?

What type of vacations are you taking? Where are you going, and with whom? For how long? How often are you taking vacations? Describe what you see, what you're doing and with whom.

What are you doing for your spouse, partner or soul mate? How are you enjoying life together? How much joy are you experiencing together? How are you growing together? How much do you love each other?

What are you doing for your kids or grandkids? What gifts have you given them? What schools are they going to? What opportunities have you been able to open up for them? How are they excelling due to your example and love? What are they saying about you?

What are you giving? How are you contributing to the world? How have you helped make it better? What programs have you funded? How much have you given? How many lives have you affected positively? How many people have you blessed? What legacy are you leaving behind?

Describe it all. What is your typical day? What time do you get up in the morning? What time do you go to bed at night? What do you do during the day? Do you work in an office? Do you work out of your home? Do you have multiple homes? Do you transact the business that you are passionate about from your home, from your computer or from wherever you are? Do you travel a lot? Do you travel around the world? What is your ideal life like?

Who are your friends? Who are your business associates? What do you typically do with them? Do you put on big events? Do you have a big sales organization? Are you recognized? Are you an author? Are you an authority? Are you a thought leader? Are you a public speaker? What do you do?

What do you do for fun? Do you play some sport or musical instrument or paint? Do you go yachting, sailing or flying in your own plane? What do you enjoy doing? Describe your life in ultimate detail. Enjoy this process.

You have all the money that you desire. You have all the success and recognition you desire. You have the great relationships. You have the health, wellness and vitality. You've accomplished everything that you desire, so what does your life look like?

And again, I am only talking here about the <u>dream</u>. I'm only talking about what the end of the story looks like. I'm not talking about how you got there. I don't want you to concern yourself for one moment about what you did to get there, or any struggles you had to overcome or anything like that. All I want you to do is to describe what your ideal life is like, what your ideal lifestyle is.

You've already worked on the foundation of this within the book, so it's time to expand on everything you've done and now at this level, with the clearing that you've already done, this should be easy. You want to take it all the way.

So right now, what's the dream? What's the dream life? Five years down the road you've attained it all, you've accomplished it all, you've achieved all of your goals, what is your life like? Who are you? Where do you live? What do you do? What do you enjoy? Describe it in ultimate detail.

Just brainstorm it now. Describe in detail in a page or two what your life is like. And if you desire to write five pages or 10, go for it. Write your Ideal Life Story and then I'm going to teach you a very, very powerful technique for taking that ideal life and making it real within your mind-body system.

So, relax and enjoy and allow your true desires to come forth. Close your eyes for a minute or two. Put your hand over your heart and allow it to speak to you and then just start writing.

Do this fun assignment now and when you're ready to put this into action and turn it into a life-long habit, I'll show you how to do it.

My Ideal Life Story

_____

_____

_____

_____

_____

_____

_____

_____

_____

_____

_____

_____

_____

_____

_____

_____

_____

_____

∽

Power Focus Session

Right now, you are going to create a very important habit, a very empowering ritual, to condition the Be It principle you learned, and this will give you the power to direct your mind on purpose. You will perform this exercise every morning to start your day, direct your focus and create a mindset that will take you where you want to go in life. You will also perform it every night right before going to sleep in order to lovingly direct your subconscious.

First of all, you must make a De Caedere decision, a commitment to start your day this way and end your day this way every day!

I know we are all busy and time is a very valuable commodity, but this habit will pay dividends that will transcend the amount of time you invest in it. The return you'll get for your time invested will, in very short order, be so much greater than the time you invest in it that it'll amaze you. The effects and return will compound over time and put you in control over your mind, your thoughts and your life and you'll never want to go back to a life without this habit.

When I started doing my first version of this ritual, which back then I called *30 Golden Minutes*, I was working both full-time during the day and part-time at night. I made the commitment to only sleep five hours a night in order to get up to do this process for 30 minutes every morning. Some people get up at 5:00 am every day to go to the gym, right? How much is your ideal life worth to you?

This is the master strategy to living an empowered life, directing your focus continually, being the most powerful version of you always to create what you desire in life every single day. Do this in a quiet place by yourself, sitting in a comfortable position with your full attention and focus on this exercise. Alternatively, if you are one of those over-busy people who feel you don't have time to even change your underwear, you can perform this exercise while you are looking in the mirror, shaving or putting on your makeup. Simply tape your exercises on your mirror and read them with passion, visualize and feel the achievement of your dreams (just don't cut yourself or smear your mascara).

Commit to giving it 20 to 30 minutes in the morning and 15 minutes at night.

1. **<u>Release Negative Emotions</u>**:

   Be aware of your feelings and release any negative emotions. Raise your vibration using one of the techniques you've learned in Step Five (Chapter 9).

2. **<u>Align with Your True Self</u>**:

   Affirm your Identity, Purpose Statement and I Am Declarations.

3. **<u>Review Your Ideal Life Story</u>**:

   You can read your Ideal Life Story aloud or to yourself, but whatever you do, read it with meaning and feeling. Put yourself, your mind and heart into the words you're reading. Words are symbolic of meaning and feeling, so really connect to each statement.

4. **<u>Focus Your Mind</u>**:

   Imagine yourself already having achieved your Ultimate Goal and living your Ideal Life Story, living your purpose in life and being the person you've decided to be.

5. **<u>Be It!</u>**

   Take it up to another level and ***really connect and feel yourself*** already having attained your vision. Squeeze your fist and state, "I Am That," to add and intensify this new state of Being It with the power and confidence of your Power Trigger! Think from this mindset and carry it with you into your day, viewing the world and acting <u>from</u> this state of consciousness.

When you finish your morning session, make a list of what you need to do today to accomplish your desired outcomes. Put them in order of priority. Your day will come together organically with your Ideal Life Story being so vivid in <u>your</u> mind.

Review your Action Blueprint and determine the actions you need to take today to put you closer to the achievement of your goal and take confident massive action.

Start your day focused, in a powerful state and committed to take the actions needed to achieve your desired results.

In the nighttime session, the goal is to flow right into sleep at the end of your session and if you fall asleep while imagining and feeling your success and happiness, that's even better. You'll look forward to going to sleep at night because you'll be giving loving instruction to your subconscious. After a while, you'll actually wake up happy and excited about your day and you'll receive inspiration and guidance from Infinite Intelligence because it communicates with you through the subconscious.

It may sound complicated if you're not used to doing it, but after a couple of weeks you'll feel very natural as it becomes a habit and you won't want to start or end your day without this ritual. Just like brushing your teeth. You will be amazed at the power this will give you. You'll start each day energized, focused and excited about life because you'll know and feel that you're in charge.

Being in control of your own life, living on purpose, will give you a tremendous amount of freedom. When your conscious and subconscious are aligned, your external world will become a mirror image of your internal world. With clear dialogue, you will be equipped to handle anything that comes up day-to-day.

Ideal Life Self-Hypnosis

I can't stress enough the importance of the Be It principle. My fascination with it, specifically how the mind works and the correlations between the conscious, subconscious and imaginative faculties led me to study hypnosis, as all of the great writers on the mind eventually bring up the topic. Before you freak out and say, "Oh no, he's gonna make me bark like a chicken," please understand that this very misunderstood experience is happening every single day to all of us. Have you ever watched TV? Have you ever played a video game? Have you ever listened to someone so boring that your mind went wandering somewhere else? Then you have been hypnotized! What does that mean? It means you went into a trance state; you had an intense focus of attention to the extent that your critical factor shut down (just like when you were young), making you totally susceptible to suggestion.

That's all being in a trance means: having an intense focus of attention so your critical factor goes to sleep (into an alpha state) and your subconscious is highly susceptible to suggestion. That's all there is to hypnosis. Let me ask you a question: why do you think that the big corporations spend millions of dollars advertising on TV? Do you think they're stupid and want to throw away large sums of money? No, they've done the studies. They know that people are in altered states of consciousness and susceptible to suggestion when they watch TV. And they are totally ready to take advantage of that fact in order to get into your pocket.

Have you ever left your house going to work and 30 minutes later you couldn't remember how you got there? Maybe you were totally absorbed in thought about some important issue or project. What was that? Who drove? You were in a trance state and your subconscious drove you there. That's its job!

Guys and girls, we're in trance states multiple times a day unconsciously. You'll either allow that to keep happening without your conscious awareness and permission or you'll learn how to do it yourself so you can direct your mind on purpose. It's that simple. Are you going to take control of your mind and direct it on purpose or are you going to let external forces with their own agenda of self-interest keep hypnotizing you without your own permission?

The easiest way to influence your subconscious mind is to suggest what you desire to it lovingly (guys) as you would treat a woman (and ladies look at it from the standpoint of how you like to be treated). To do this you get in a relaxed and receptive state and imagine and feel that what you desire to be already is. Be it! It's that simple! To do this you must learn a strategy to get yourself into a very relaxed state so you can focus, vividly imagine and feel your most cherished desires are already yours. The more certainty you feel that you are, do or have what you desire, the quicker it will manifest in the material world.

So let me teach you how to hypnotize yourself. Don't freak out, it's no big deal. It's happening to you multiple times a day without your permission for other people's gain. Might as well do it to yourself with your own permission for the purposes you desire for your own personal gain. It's really very easy!

My mentor in hypnosis, Igor Ledochowski, creator of *The Power of Conversational Hypnosis,* is a master hypnotist who has developed very powerful programs that have helped thousands of people overcome many issues through hypnosis. My personal studies on the topic centered strongly on self-hypnosis, as I was interested in affecting significant changes in myself and as always, teaching others how to use it to transform their lives. Igor has created a very effective and simple model, which he taught me to help anyone hypnotize themselves. It's based on the acronym CAVE.

C: Confirm
A: Affirm
V: Visualize
E: Effortless Flow

What this means is that you get yourself into a relaxed state and use a physical sensation to *confirm* that you are in a trance or alpha state of consciousness. We're going to use our left arm and get it very relaxed as a means of your knowing or *confirming* that you're in a trance or alpha state. Then once you're there you will *affirm* and *visualize*, that's the A and V in our formula to affirm what you desire and visualize it. Then, finally, prior to coming out of this relaxed state you'll just allow your consciousness to drift into an *effortless flow*, like you're floating downstream on a calm river. Now instead of directing your thought, you let it flow so that your subconscious can assimilate the suggestion you've just given it. This actually mirrors the process you'd go through <u>prior to and while falling</u> asleep. This is why it is so important in directing your subconscious that you have your intentions clearly in mind and feel as if they're already fulfilled before falling asleep, so that your instructions to it are to manifest these desires in your material world.

Now, I have a special gift for you. Go to http://CarlosMarin.com/usf and create an account. When you're ready, click on Audio and then click *Ideal Life Meditation* to let me guide you through the Power Focus Session meditation to produce amazing results today and in the future! [Once you have created an account, a temporary password will be emailed to you. Thereafter, you can access all bonus content through the login page at http://usfbook.carlosmarin.com/login. Simply enter your email and password.]

If you'll start and end your day, every day, with this exercise, it won't be long before you'll find yourself directing your mind consistently and effortlessly. You will find yourself at a point where you'll *love the process*, and when you do that, you're on the road to mastery. You see, mastery requires that you love the process, and the process requires loving repetition and as I've told you from the beginning, your subconscious loves repetition.

If you will commit to performing this exercise every morning and night for the next 30 days, I promise you the results will surprise and delight you. You'll never go back to what you did before. You'll be hooked because you'll gain control of your mind and your thoughts, which control your actions, create your habits and you will create the future of your dreams automatically!

Chapter 13

BONUS STEPS: GET A MENTOR AND USE A SYSTEM

The mediocre teacher tells. The good teacher explains. The superior teacher demonstrates. The great teacher inspires.

—**William Arthur Ward**

The Yoda Factor

For many years, and as is evident in this book, I've been a big fan of the *Star Wars* movies due to the entertaining manner with which they teach success principles. I've been particularly enamored with the way the Jedi (which represent all of the wisdom traditions of mankind) teach their very best students to become the best they can be through a

212

system of mentoring by the most powerful teachers, the Jedi Knights. All through the ages this has been the most highly effective way to develop super achievers and systematic mentoring is the only shortcut there is to success.

The Power of Mentors and Systems

As I've said from the very beginning of this book and you learned in detail in the previous chapter, the secret to achieving anything is going to Point B and adopting the mindset of the person who already has what you desire. This is why you should continually read about and study people who have what you want in life, and model them in that area. Human beings learn by modeling. It's our preferred learning strategy.

Children learn by modeling those around them, which is what we all do. Monkey see, monkey do — that's our hereditary programming! So, the way to save a lot of time, trouble and heartache is to model people who have what you want and are where you want to be. You can do it with people you know personally and people you don't know but can read about. That's the magic of the mentor.

My grandfather told me about mentors when I was young but I became cynical when I started in the business world. I believed that no one would share their secret to success because I believed there was a limited supply of wealth and who would want to lose what they had to help someone else?

Afterwards, when I had the chance to work closely with multi-millionaires who were willing to freely share their wealth strategies, the lights went on in my head. I jumped on the opportunity and came to realize that having a mentor meant all the difference in the world.

Study the Best

The best and fastest way to learn to think accurately is to find an accurate thinker who has the results you want to achieve, or at least is on the way to achieving it and is ahead of you on the path, and model that person.

Record this belief indelibly in your mind and live by it, "If any person in this world can produce a result, I can produce the same result if I create the same mindset, use the same strategies and intensity of action!"

Last year, while I was editing my book, I found the brilliant young man who I told you about earlier, Brendon Burchard. He is the foremost strategist in online marketing, so I went to one of his events, Experts Academy, and was so impressed by his knowledge that I decided I wanted him to be my mentor. I joined his Center Ring, his highest-level mastermind group, in order to be able to study him and learn his mindset and strategies. I calculate that his mentoring will produce 10x results in my businesses in the next couple of years. I highly recommend his programs as well as his books, *The Millionaire Messenger* and *The Charge,* to any entrepreneur that is serious about their success and looking to take their lives to a whole new level. I know it has for me!

To create your best life you must become a student of the principles of success. From this day forward listen to audios, read books and attend seminars from people who have produced the results you desire. Then, apply the principles by taking action on them. Remember, none of us are demonstrating perfection (yet!) in all areas, but model them in the area of life in which they're successful and that you want to emulate.

Become a student of accurate thinking. Become a seeker of wisdom. Develop accurate principle-based beliefs that will empower you to attract all of life's riches automatically.

18th century German poet and writer, Johann Wolfgang von Goethe, stated, "Before you can do something, you must first be something." In other words, you have to *be* in order to *do* and *do* in order to *have*. It's the same with all of us. You cannot give what you don't have. So be careful and make sure the people you model have what you want before you listen to them.

One of my mentors, Jim Rohn, the great American philosopher and author of *The Five Major Pieces of the Life Puzzle*, passed away in 2009. Jim was incredibly wise and I loved bringing him in to talk to my organizations as often as possible. I think he must have seen the hunger for knowledge and wisdom that I had the first time I had him in to speak, and before leaving he turned and said to me, "Carlos, if you'll invest as much time working on yourself as you do on your business, you'll have all the success and wealth you could ever desire!" I never forgot what he said that day and I took it to heart. Am I ever glad I took his advice because it has paid huge dividends! When people ask me what I'm the best at, my response is always, "I'm the best student!"

What is this book about, if not modeling success? Once you've finished it, to generate the results you want you must follow through on everything you learned here and turn it into a habit. I feel very blessed that I was able to find mentors that taught me so many powerful principles that transformed my life and I hope that you will consider me as your mentor. It would be my honor and privilege to help you create everything you desire in your life.

My purpose is to inspire and empower hundreds of millions of people to know their true inner power and use it to be free and manifest their dreams. I also know how the universe works and whatever I give is multiplied many times and returned to me. Therefore, I bless you and God blesses me.

Franchise Systems

A big part of the business success I've enjoyed for almost 30 years has come from creating and using franchise type business building systems to develop massive sales organizations. These systems have generated several billion dollars in revenues for the companies and sales organizations I created them for and even continue to be used in places where I haven't worked in years. Most recently, I developed a business building system for a company that has grown from start-up to over $1 billion in annual sales in seven years. This is the power of systems.

What I'm doing in this book and in the system I've created that I teach in my live events and video training programs is taking the same concept of a franchise-type business system and applying it to personal development. After all, if it will work in business generating that much success, it will work in the individual lives of people doing whatever it is they do!

It is the concept of taking what is proven to work in a principle-based manner and chunking it down into easy-to-assimilate bite sized pieces. Then you create a paint-by-numbers, step-by-step, duplicable process that anyone can follow, and teach it to people to produce consistent, predictable, successful results. That is the power of mentors and systems.

Epilogue

AUTOMATING YOUR NEW MINDSET

Whatever results you're producing in your life you are doing automatically. If you want new and better results, change your mindset and you will produce them...automatically.

—Carlos Marin

I'm not going to call this the end because this is actually a new beginning. You are about to complete this book and embark on a fantastic journey, a fun-filled adventure called: Your Life Lived on Purpose.

It's a story you will write, produce, direct and star in. It will be the most joyous, exciting story of success, achievement, wealth, fame, contribution and fulfillment that you've ever seen — because it's all about you.

This is your story as <u>decided by you</u>, not by your parents, friends, siblings, boss or your past conditioning. This is you creating your own destiny. There's nothing more exciting than knowing that you're in charge and can create and live life according to your own desires, dreams and aspirations.

Keep developing your abilities and creating empowering habit patterns, something you've been learning all along in the book but now you'll do it consciously, so you live up to your potential and realize our own greatness.

Go the extra mile and become indispensable. You create good will and people will want to be around you and do business with you over and over and over again.

Give Empowering Meaning

As you embark on your journey to create your destiny in life, remember that problems and challenges will arise along the way. But I'd like you to realize something that's taken me years to understand. The problems or challenges that arise at every stage of life represent a lesson we need to learn at that time. There's a major benefit within the solution to the problem, a benefit that will get you closer to your dreams.

If you suffer a misstep, get stuck or lose your way, focus on the solution and ask yourself:

1. What's great about this problem?
2. What can I learn from this problem that will take my life to the next level?
3. What is the opportunity hidden in this problem?

4. How can I create a solution that will take me to where I want to go?

When you do this, you'll start thanking God for your problems and you'll receive a better quality problem each time. Each one will take you higher and closer to where you want to go.

Remember, you can give empowering meaning to anything that happens. It's impossible to fail as long as you persist. You only fail once you've given up! So failure is really impossible.

Beliefs to Live By

What I've done with you in this book is what I did with myself to completely turn my life around and go from being broke, unhappy and unfulfilled to being wealthy, happy and fulfilling my life's purpose while living my dreams.

These are some of the beliefs that I adopted or developed as my own, by choice and on purpose. They have empowered me to transform my life and I highly recommend you adopt them as your own:

- I am one with God and His unlimited power within me, which continually manifests my intentions easily, quickly and automatically.
- I live each moment in an attitude of appreciation and gratitude for all my blessings and the beauty and grandeur of the universe.
- I look for the best in all people, conditions and circumstances.

- Every problem contains the seed of a greater benefit and is a stepping-stone to the achievement of my dreams.
- The bigger the problem, the better the solution, the bigger the reward.
- Nothing in life has any meaning except the meaning I give it.
- I give empowering meaning to everything that happens.
- I direct my focus; I shape my reality and manifest my dreams.
- I create my own future by design and inspiration!
- I have the potential, ability and power to be, do and have whatever I desire.
- I'm totally responsible for my results in life.
- Everything happens for a reason and that reason serves me.
- Whatever I conceive and believe I can achieve.
- If it's to be, it's up to me.
- I may not have the most talent but I can outwork anybody.
- There is no such thing as failure, only success or learning.
- There is always a way if I'm committed.
- I hold myself to a higher standard than anyone else does.
- It's not what I achieve but who I become in the process of achieving.
- I am master over my thoughts, mind and emotions.
- If I can't I must, if I must then I can.
- The universe is conspiring to give me everything I desire.

As you can imagine, with this belief system you feel empowered almost all of the time and can reframe everything that occurs to direct your focus on purpose get your Point B results consistently and automatically.

Stay in Touch

I sincerely hope you've enjoyed our time together as much as I have. I encourage you to make a lifelong commitment to learning, improving and evolving. Turbo-charge your journey in personal transformation and the corresponding riches that come with them by joining me at some of my live programs soon. I guarantee you'll have a blast and your level of belief, awareness and results will skyrocket. You can check our event schedule at http://carlosmarin.com/events or by clicking on the Events tab at CarlosMarin.com.

I truly wish you success, wealth, health, happiness and fulfillment as you make your mark on this world. I'd love to read about your accomplishments and your success story.

Please share them with me:

Facebook at http://facebook.com/CarlosMarinLive
Twitter at http://twitter.com/CarlosMarinLive
Email at info@carlosmarin.com

Please visit my website at http://carlosmarin.com and sign up to receive free training, reports and videos I provide there for my subscribers. Also sign up for my 21-Day Success Challenge at http://carlosmarin.com/21eng to maximize your productivity, own your life and achieve your goals in record time!

Check out my videos on YouTube at
http://YouTube.com/CarlosMarinTV.

I believe that you and I are kindred spirits. We are all part of a God that wants to bless us with anything and everything we can imagine and then some.

I'm sure our paths will cross again, but until then, my last assignment for you is this:

Shine your light on the world. Make your mark.
Bless the rest of mankind with your gifts and talents.
We all need you and your greatness!
Keep transforming yourself. Live the potential that God
created you to be and receive your automatic riches!

I wish you all the best in life and…

MAY GOD BLESS YOU AND
YOUR LOVED ONES ALWAYS!!!

ABOUT THE AUTHOR

For over 30 years Carlos Marin has built sales and marketing networks that have recruited and trained several million entrepreneurs while generating billions of dollars in sales revenues throughout North America, South America and Western Europe.

Using this huge enterprise as a laboratory to test success philosophies and principles, Carlos developed a system of training and education that truly empowers people; helping them to achieve their goals by overcoming their conditioned limitations and beliefs. His principle-based philosophy is built on Universal Principles that show people how to access the unlimited potential that already resides within them and how to use this inner power to achieve the success, wealth, freedom and happiness they desire in their lives.

Carlos's system utilizes audios, videos, live events and multi-media Internet content to deliver his life transforming messages and tools. He is a powerful, dynamic and entertaining speaker who has shared the stage with such greats as Denis Waitley, Jim Rohn, Brian Tracy, Zig

Ziglar, Les Brown, John Maxwell, Bob Burg, Larry Wilson, Ronald Reagan, General Norman Schwarzkopf, Miguel Angel Cornejo, Alex Day, and Camilo Cruz among many others.

Carlos has trained his audiences in universal success principles, personal and organizational excellence, goal achievement, changing limiting belief systems, leadership skills, public speaking, effective communications, sales and marketing, and the recruiting, training and building of large marketing organizations.

Over one million people have attended his live events, which included the largest ever in Latin America where over 67,000 people attended a 2-day motivational event at the University of Mexico Olympic Stadium. His audios and videos have sold well over ten million copies in both English and Spanish.

Most recently, Carlos created a web-based Video Centric Marketing, Recruiting and Training system for a Texas energy company that helped take them from start-up to over $1 billion in annual revenues in 7 years.

Carlos is a Certified Hypnotherapist and an NLP and EFT Master. His Personal Empowerment system, which has been proven over time, has helped over one hundred entrepreneurs become millionaires, and has evolved over the last 5 years into the Unlimited Success Academy.

RESOURCES

Experts

The experts listed in this section are prominent Thought Leaders, and are some of my current mentors in various key areas of success or life. They are listed here by chapter as they appear in this book, along with the titles of some of their books, products and specific areas of expertise. Their main website has also been listed for ease of accessing them and their products and services, which I highly recommend you do.

Foreword
Jack Canfield: *Chicken Soup for the Soul, The Success Principles;* Bestselling Author, Personal Life Coach, Psychologist, Founder of The Transformational Leadership Council, America's #1 Success Coach
http://jackcanfield.com

Acknowledgements
John C. Maxwell: *The 21 Irrefutable Laws of Leadership, Thinking for a Change;* Author, Speaker, Success Trainer, Global Thought Leader, Renowned Leadership Expert
http://johnmaxwell.com

Chapter 2

Bob Proctor: *You Were Born Rich*, and numerous personal development programs; Philosopher, Speaker, Law of Attraction Expert, Global Thought Leader
http://proctorgallagherinstitute.com

Bruce H. Lipton, PhD: *The Biology of Belief;* Stem Cell Biologist, Global Leader in Bridging Science and Spirit, Speaker, Author
http://BruceLipton.com

Chapter 4

Anthony Robbins: *Awaken the Giant Within, Unlimited Power;* Peak Performance Coach, Personal Transformation Expert, Life Coach, Motivational Speaker, Global Thought Leader
http://Tonyrobbins.com

Brendon Burchard: *The Charge, The Millionaire Messenger;* Bestselling Author, Speaker, Global Thought Leader, High-Performance Trainer, Founder of Experts Academy, Online Marketing Guru
http://Brendonburchard.com

Chapter 6

Janet Bray Attwood and Chris Attwood: *The Passion Test;* Bestselling Authors, Speakers, Empowerment Leaders
http://thepassiontest.com

Marcia Wieder: *Making Your Dreams Come True, Doing Less and Having More;* Author, Charismatic and Inspirational Speaker, Dream Coach
http://marciawieder.com

Chapter 9

Hale Dwoskin: *The Sedona Method;* Best Selling Author, Founder of *Sedona* Training Associates, International Speaker, Emotional Well-Being Expert, Success Leader
http://sedona.com

Shawn Achor: *The Happiness Advantage;* Best Selling Author, Psychologist, Happiness Expert, Success Trainer, Motivational Speaker
http://goodthinkinc.com

Chapter 10

Alex Mandossian: *TeleSeminar Secrets and Virtual Book Tour Secrets;* Online Marketing Expert, Founder of MarketingOnline.com, Author, Trainer, Speaker, Productivity Expert
http://alexmandossian.com

Brian Tracy: *Flight Plan- The Real Secret of Success;* Bestselling Author, Professional Speaker, Entrepreneur, Success Expert, Business Trainer
http://briantracy.com

Experts Industry Association: Association of Experts dedicated to educating and training people worldwide to achieve success by following their passion to share their knowledge with mankind
http://expertsindustryassociation.com

Chapter 11

Denis Waitley: *10 Seeds of Greatness, The Psychology of Winning;* Bestselling Author, Success Expert, High Performance and Productivity Consultant, Keynote Lecturer, Member of Speaker's Hall of Fame
http://waitley.com

Chapter 12

Mary Morrissey: *Quantum Leap Program;* International Speaker, Best Selling Author, CEO Consultant, Visionary, Empowerment Specialist
http://marymorrissey.com

Igor Ledochowski: *Power of Conversational Hypnosis;* World Famous Certified Master Hypnotist and Trainer, NLP Master

Practitioner, Certified Success Life Coach, Author, Mentor
http://igorledochowski.com

Recommended Reading

The following list contains many of the books that have shaped my
mindset and thinking processes over the last 30 years. It is not meant
to be an exhaustive list of everything I've read, simply many of the best
and most transformative books that are coherent with the principles
in this book to create positive change quickly in your life.

Anthony Robbins	*Awaken the Giant Within*
	Unlimited Power
Bob Proctor	*You Were Born Rich*
Brendon Burchard	*The Charge*
	The Millionaire Messenger
Brian Tracy	*Flight Plan- The Real Secret of Success*
Bruce H. Lipton, PhD	*The Biology of Belief*
Carlos Marin	*The Ultimate Success Formula*
Catherine Ponder	*The Dynamic Laws of Prosperity*
Charles F. Haanel	*The Master Key System*
Claude M. Bristol	*The Magic of Believing*
David Schwartz, PhD	*The Magic of Thinking Big*
	The Magic of Self Direction
Deepak Chopra	*The Seven Spiritual Laws of Success*
Denis Waitley	*The Psychology of Winning*
	10 Seeds of Greatness
Don Miguel Ruiz	*The Four Agreements*
Eckhart Tolle	*The Power of Now*
Ernest Holmes	*Creative Mind and Success*

Florence Scovel Shinn	*The Game of Life And How To Play It*
	The Power of the Spoken Word
Glenn Bland	*Success! The Glenn Bland Method*
Hale Dwoskin	*The Sedona Method*
Igor Ledochowski	*The Power of Conversational Hypnosis*
	(7 CD Program w/ 412 pg. manual)
Jack Canfield	*The Success Principles*
	The Power of Focus
Jack Canfield	*Tapping Into Ultimate Success*
and Pamela Bruner	
James Allen	*As A Man Thinketh*
Janet Bray Attwood	*The Passion Test: The Effortless Path to*
and Chris Attwood	*Discovering Your Life's Purpose*
Janet Lowe	*Bill Gates Speaks*
Jim Rohn	*The Five Major Pieces to the Life Puzzle*
	7 Strategies for Wealth & Happiness
Joe Vitale	*The Attractor Factor*
John C. Maxwell	*The 21 Irrefutable Laws of Leadership*
	Thinking for a Change
John Randolph Price	*The Abundance Book*
Jose Silva	*The Silva Mind Control Method*
Joseph Murphy, PhD	*Think Yourself Rich*
	The Power of Your Subconscious Mind
Les Giblin	*How to Have Power and Confidence*
	in Dealing with People
Marcia Wieder	*Making Your Dreams Come True*
Mary Morrissey	*Building Your Field of Dreams*
Maxwell Maltz	*Psycho-Cybernetics*
Napoleon Hill	*Think and Grow Rich*
	The Master Key to Riches

Neville Goddard	*The Power of Awareness*
	The Law and the Promise
Nick Ortner	*The Tapping Solution*
Norman Vincent Peale	*The Power of Positive Thinking*
	Positive Imaging
Rhonda Byrne	*The Secret*
Scott Thorpe	*How to Think Like Einstein*
Shawn Achor	*The Happiness Advantage*
	Before Happiness
Stephen R. Covey	*The 7 Habits of Highly Effective People*
Thomas Troward	*The Edinburgh and Dore Lectures on Mental Science*
	The Creative Process in the Individual
Wallace Wattles	*The Science of Getting Rich*
Wayne W. Dyer	*The Power of Intention*
	Your Erroneous Zones

CPSIA information can be obtained at www.ICGtesting.com
Printed in the USA
LVOW07s1413051114

412002LV00005B/5/P